Inside the TV Writer's Room

Practical Advice for Succeeding in Television

Edited by **Lawrence Meyers**

Syracuse University Press

∞ The paper used in this publication meets the minimum requirements
of the American National Standard for Information Sciences—Permanence
of Paper for Printed Library Materials, ANSI Z39.48-1992.

For a listing of books published and distributed by Syracuse University Press,
visit our Web site at SyracuseUniversityPress.syr.edu.

ISBN: 978-0-8156-3241-2

Library of Congress Cataloging-in-Publication Data

Inside the TV writers' room : practical advice for succeeding in television /
edited by Lawrence Meyers. — 1st ed.
    p. cm. — (Television and popular culture)
  Includes bibliographical references and index.
  ISBN 978-0-8156-3241-2 (cloth : alk. paper)
 1. Television authorship.   I. Meyers, Lawrence.
  PN1992.7I53 2010
  808'.066791—dc22   2010007084

Manufactured in the United States of America

For Amanda and Jessica

Lawrence Meyers is a veteran writer-producer of episodic television, financial journalist, and entrepreneur in the field of consumer finance. His first book, *Teacher of the Year: The Mystery and Legacy of Edwin Barlow,* was published in 2009. He resides in Los Angeles.

Contents

Preface

The interviews that appear in this book were actually conducted individually, but I edited the book to create a "virtual roundtable," in which the participants sound off on each topic simultaneously rather than individually.

I've suggested some television episodes to view for each chapter, which is best done prior to reading the text. Some episodes are written by the participants, some are reflective of what is discussed in the chapter, and some are just examples of great television writing. The goal here is not to provide the reader with television shows that explicitly demonstrate what is discussed, but to slowly build a gestalt of what makes good television over the course of the book.

I also suggest some further reading at the end of each chapter, for those readers who are inclined to investigate some of the lessons further. Not all the readings are directly applicable to the chapter in which they appear, but they do provide essential insights into the art.

Each chapter ostensibly provides real-world "how-to" experience, but ends with a lesson delving deeper into the chapter's subject. The goal is to understand why things are the way they are, and how it all impacts the writer.

I would like to acknowledge all the participants for their time and the honesty presented in the interviews, as well as friends, family, and colleagues for their valuable input.

Be sure to visit **www.thewritersroom.tv** and **www.tvwritersroom.com** for additional content, including unpublished interviews and advice on seeking a career in television writing.

Introduction

Judging by the 563 listings on Amazon.com under the search term *Writing for Television*, aspiring television writers are asking how to break into the television business. They are asking the wrong question.

The real answer to knowing *how* is to ask *why* and *what*. *Why* do people become writers, and *what* makes them successful?

Books about writing in the entertainment industry focus exclusively on "how to" do something (for example, "How to Break into Hollywood," "How to Write a Screenplay"). Yet "how to" do anything is irrelevant when you are not even sure *why* you are doing something in the first place. The questions of "why" are what this book is about.

By charging directly to instruction on how to do something (when there is no one "right" way, anyway), these publications do a disservice by focusing on product, which is transitory. Yes, it will survive the author and live on for audiences. However, for the author, process is the coal that fuels the artistic soul, providing invaluable and eternal lessons that will be drawn upon for each succeeding work.

Each chapter contains a discussion between myself and established television writers—someone in the trenches of network television. I delve into areas few artists have taken the time to explore themselves—the psychological and spiritual areas that demonstrate how their creative process developed, how it survives, and how they became successful.

These discussions focus on the intangible drive within the writer's soul to express oneself, how each writer explored and honed his or her creativity, the compromises they've made to nurture it both prior to finding success and after, how they draw upon creativity when they are confronted with the inelastic deadlines of network television, how they cope with the collision of artistic fulfillment and the harsh realities of commerce, and how they inject personal feelings and an original voice into a show that is often not of their own making.

Every reader should find at least one writer to identify with because the participants have been culled from every conceivable background: geographical base, family situation, ethnicity, educational accomplishment, prior profession, gender, age, and professional experience. The book includes writers from shows that run the gamut from *Law & Order* to *Star Trek*, from *CSI: Miami* to *Boston Public*, and from *Judging Amy* to *Lost*. Most important, each writer is a down-to-earth, regular person that any reader would enjoy spending time with (I know I did).

The book is not just for writers, however. It has been carefully crafted to throw open the gates of Hollywood to average television viewers, who crave understanding of how their favorite shows coalesce each week and elevate writers to cult status. This book is as much for the nonwriter as it is for the professional scribe.

Inside the TV Writer's Room

1

How to Break In; or, Why It's All So Random

"How did you break into the business?"

This question is the one most frequently asked of Hollywood writers. The good news is there is a common answer to that question. The bad news is that the answer provides no guidance, secret method, or magical handshake that permits one to gain entrance to this exclusive fraternity.

I'll provide the answer at the end of the chapter, if you don't guess it on your own. I'll also give you a hint. As you read, focus not on what the participants say about how they got into the business but what the nature of the business reveals about itself.

Suggested Viewings

ER: "Hell & High Water," by Neal Baer
The Shield: "Family Meeting," by Shawn Ryan
Boomtown: "Insured by Smith & Wesson," teleplay by Chris Brancato

LARRY: Chris, you came into Hollywood from an obscure angle.

CHRIS BRANCATO: I flirted for one second with Wall Street, made money and figured it would support my writing career later. But I'm an idiot when it comes to economics. Somehow I lucked into a job as Warren Beatty's assistant. I was the assistant there for postproduction on *Ishtar* [1994]. It was incredible, learning the world of a movie star. It gave me some contacts, none of which specifically helped my career but just put me into the business.

LARRY: Was there any one particular big lesson you learned from Warren?

1

CHRIS: Despite being in the company of Warren Beatty, I could see regular people involved in the creative process and trying to tell a story. I realized it was not rocket science.

LARRY: And how did you actually become a writer?

CHRIS: By writing scripts!

LARRY: When came the decision that "this is what I want to do"?

CHRIS: It was more a lack of other options. I was not good at other jobs. I managed a restaurant—I got fired. I did this—I got fired. I did that—got fired. I did not have the energy or interest in anything other than pursuing screenwriting once that bug had bitten me. When I got out of college I did not know what kind of writing I was going to do. My mother was in the Writers Guild, and this pamphlet said the pay for an hour script was twenty-two thousand dollars! That clinched it. I had to ultimately pay for that because my writing suffered. The interest in it was purely mercenary. Only when it became a little more personal and deeper, that's when I started to sell stuff.

LARRY: Jane, your career start is a case of passion driving you so hard that you literally wrote your way into the business.

JANE ESPENSON: I started writing spec episodes of *Star Trek: The Next Generation*, of which I was a fan. I loved the Data character—I could have anything happen to Data—so I wrote three specs, and sent the last and best one in.

LARRY: *Trek* was really the only show that allowed unsolicited scripts.

JANE: I got a phone call saying, "We love the script. We want you to come in and pitch." I was thrilled, made an appointment, told them I'll be there—and had no idea what a pitch was. But I figured it out, went in, and they bought something. It did not get produced, but I started ignoring my graduate studies, to concentrate on getting my pitches ready for the next pitch session.

LARRY: So they invited you back?

JANE: Yeah. I sold another thing, then later wrote a spec sitcom, which an executive involved with the Disney Fellowship program liked. I got into the fellowship, quit grad school in Berkeley, and moved here.

LARRY: How did it feel?

JANE: I was having panic attacks. I'd sat in college ten years, not just because I loved college but because it was very safe for me. But now I was so close to my dream and if it did not pay off, that would be it. Dream gone. Terrifying. But as soon as I got there I started feeling better. I pitched some ideas to the show *Dinosaurs* [ABC], I got to sit in the Writers' Room although they produced an episode, and then they did not kick me out.

LARRY: The show had been canceled, so why not keep you?

JANE: Exactly. They knew there were only a few more to write so I got to join the writers for those. I became a de facto member of the *Dinosaurs* staff and got my first agent. After that, one show just led to another, despite the fact that they all got canceled pretty quickly, and I knew I was not doing great at it.

LARRY: Sitcoms are hard work.

JANE: I was so intimidated by the funny people around me. The Room was just really funny, overlapping and loud and crass and crude and very male, and I was not thriving. Then the work kind of dried up. So I contacted everyone I knew to see if I could get a freelance. And I got two serial dramas that year. I wrote an episode of *Nowhere Man* and one of *Star Trek*.

LARRY: It really seems to be a matter of getting a good script read by the right person at the right time. Javier, you actually snuck in from the executive suite.

JAVIER GRILLO-MARXUACH: I got a message from USC, where I'd gone to film school, that NBC was looking for somebody with a screenwriting degree to enter the executive training program. The thought was that they would find people who had experience with writing that could communicate with writers. But I did not want to do television. Television? Ugh. I'm a *screen*writer—I write for the screen! But I got this opportunity and thought, "Let's give it a shot." Part of it was that they printed the starting salary in the job announcement, and I really needed the money to buy a laser-disc player.

LARRY: So—with apologies to our mutual friends at the networks—with very little knowledge of television, you became a network executive!

JAVIER: It was like going to grad school all over again. I was put in a situation where I was a prime-time series executive working on stuff that was on the air! I fell in love with television. Meanwhile, I had friends who'd sold screenplays, and horror stories were trickling down of how screenwriters were treated.

LARRY: And you've been reading tons of TV scripts and getting a handle on how to do it and what works and what doesn't.

JAVIER: I was involved in the hands-on side of the industry. It eventually dawned on me that there were decisions that I made that actually had repercussions on something that showed up on the air!

LARRY: So how did you end up writing on *SeaQuest: DSV*?

JAVIER: It's a roundabout story. Because my father's an oncologist, my entire life I've been told that cigarettes are literally Satan's tools on earth. But when I did theater in college I learned to be a social smoker because it was the best way to communicate to the actors: If there was a difficult note I had to give them, right? I'd call a break and bum a smoke, and then I was not the director anymore, just a guy saying, "Hey, maybe you should try this." Okay, now flash-forward to working as a network current executive on *SeaQuest*. The executive producer had been very tough on me because I was young and not entirely nonignorant. We were coming back from the set, and he asked me if I wanted to have a drink, and I said, "Sure." I don't drink either, but you don't turn down an invite from the showrunner! So I went and ordered a Scotch, and he pulls out his cigarettes and said, "Would you like a cigarette?" And I'm like, "Absolutely, I would. Thank you, sir. May I have another?" And we're smoking and we're drinking, and I'm sick as hell.

LARRY: With the voice of your oncologist father pounding in your head, "Caaaancerrrr."

JAVIER: Damn right. And the showrunner says to me, "Kid, you're going to be running the network in a couple of years." I said, "Well, actually I trained to be a writer, and that's what I want to do." And in this completely bizarro random moment of generosity, he says, "If the show gets picked up for a third season, I'll make you a staff writer."

LARRY: So you're thinking it's a trick?

JAVIER: Nobody expected the show to get picked up. Then their troubles began because the show got picked up for a third season, and I promptly quit NBC and went to work for *SeaQuest*.

LARRY: Any other stories of just brute-force determination?

HART HANSON: I was driven totally by financial need to raise my family. There was a show shot on the West Coast called *The Beachcombers* for the CBC, a half-hour drama, which was on the air for [nineteen] years.

LARRY: What was it about?

HART: Two guys who fight for logs. I'm not kidding. Instead of two people shooting each other, it was about two boats fighting for logs. The show went on so long that the principals just died. I faxed in a million ideas until they gave me a script, then I became head writer, then I created my own shows.

LARRY: Well, I want to move to Canada. Jason, one of my all-time favorite shows was *My So-Called Life*. How'd you end up there?

JASON KATIMS: I had written a short ten-minute play. I got a phone call from Ed Zwick, and he said, "I read a play of yours and enjoyed it." I said, "Oh, thank you." He said, "Do you know who I am?" I said, "No." He said, "Well, I'll just list a few things."

LARRY: D'OH!

JASON: Serves me right. And he said, "If you have any interest in writing for television, I want to talk to you about it." So I got on a plane. They were developing *My So-Called Life*. It was early in the process, and I got to see the drafts, and I was there when they shot the pilot. So they gave me a script. I could not have had a better experience of entering this world because I was literally working with the best people on this very special show. The only problem was it was intimidating.

LARRY: Did they have to teach you the whole TV structure, or were you aware of it already?

JASON: I was not aware of it. I just read many scripts, and they sent me outlines from *thirtysomething* and then the script, and then I'd have the tape so I would get to see the process. They had all these great people there like Winnie Holzman and Richard Kramer and Ed and Marshall and Scott Winant. It was like my graduate school.

LARRY: Tim, you slid in from the production side, right?

TIM KRING: Yes and no. I never even thought about writing scripts when I got out of film school. I pulled cables and shot some documentaries. I finally got a gig with a commercial house where I would come on with a camera crew as a second assistant shooting Japanese cigarette commercials. I had an opportunity to get into the camera crew and decided I did not really want to do that with my life. So I sat down and wrote a script and went back to all the people I had met, got an agent out of it, and started going out on a gazillion pitch meetings and pitched anything I could.

LARRY: Back in the days when those sorts of meetings were more ubiquitous.

TIM: Yes. My first job was writing an episode of *Knight Rider,* and it was really one of those things where I got hired on Tuesday and they needed it the following Thursday and I had a check for seventeen thousand dollars two weeks later. I thought, "This is unbelievable. How did I do this and where did this come from and how could they pay me this much money?" It was really staggering.

LARRY: All this pitching, obviously, you got better at story. It sounds like it's all self-taught.

TIM: I never once traded on my education at USC, not once. Nor did I ever learn anything about how to be a writer. Ninety percent of it was sitting in a room with people and pitching ideas and taking their notes.

LARRY: So after *Knight Rider*'s big check, you wanted to get more.

TIM: I did not know any other legal way you could make that kind of money. My father made forty-nine thousand dollars a year, and I just made seventeen thousand in a week. I wrote as much as I could, and for many, many years I was a freelance writer.

LARRY: So you did this for, then, years?

TIM: My first job was in 1985. I went onto *Chicago Hope* as a series producer and a writer in 1996.

LARRY: Frank, how did the door open for you?

FRANK MILITARY: I made student films at Northwestern and placed second in a national competition. The Motion Picture Academy flew me out, and an agency signed me.

LARRY: And once you got an agent, you were in.

FRANK: Then the legendary Larry Turman optioned a script, and he flew me out here to meet Michael Apted. I had done some acting in college. Michael Mann then cast me in *Vice*, and then he invited me to do a script for him. After that, work came my way.

LARRY: Vanessa, how did you break in?

VANESSA TAYLOR: I wanted to get a writer's assistant job. I wrote a letter to Rob Thomas, who just had *Cupid* picked up. "Hey, Rob. I'd really like to be your assistant. I'm interested in the work you are doing." And lo and behold, he hired me. At Christmas, I asked for half a script, and he gave me that. Then I asked him to put me on staff. He did that.

LARRY: Where you met Hart Hanson?

VANESSA: Hart got me a meeting with his agent, with whom I ended up signing.

LARRY: Shawn, you had what some would call a start-and-stop approach to Hollywood.

SHAWN RYAN: I just turned twenty-three, and got a freelance on the sitcom *My Two Dads*. For the first three or four days I don't think I said a word. Bob Meyer was running the show, and he was a constant pro; it was great. There was a guy there who'd written for *Happy Days*, and I thought that was the coolest thing. The second week I actually talked a little bit. I'll never forget them going through a script, and they were talking and something just made me blurt out a joke that I love and they actually liked it and used it. So my very first contribution to television was a totally unaccredited joke and rewrite.

LARRY: Did you try for more with them?

SHAWN: I helped them come up with another episode, and that turned out to be my first screen credit. Then I could not get any writing work for four and a half years.

LARRY: But fate brought you back.

SHAWN: I found myself on *Nash Bridges* for three years. I tried really hard to prove myself, and what I realized very early on was that the job as a staff writer was much more than writing a script. I knew I was going to get rewritten, so what was my edge? I made myself valuable to them by helping come up with stories.

LARRY: Bob, you told me that you caddied for the late Dan Curtis, the creator of *Dark Shadows*. Was that how you got started?

ROBERT SINGER: Yes, he was doing his second *Dark Shadows* movie, and I was the gofer. Dan was great, and he kept me on with him after the picture ended, and I started to learn about development. I would sit in his office in New York and read books looking for material. And then a couple years later, we did a Movie of the Week, and he decided to move to California and took me with him. To this day, Dan called me "Kid." So it was always "Kid." I think some part of Dan always thought of me that way. And although he always wanted me to do well and had nothing but the best wishes for me, it really was not until I left Dan that I was able to become an adult. Really, he kicked me out of the nest. He said, "If you want to succeed, it's not going to be here with me because where are you going to go?" He called everybody in town on my behalf.

LARRY: So you had been steeped in production with Dan, and knew that whole angle.

ROBERT: More than I realized. I took a job with Larry Gordon producing a pilot and joined him when he only had a writer and director. I went out and found production space and hired all the people for this job. I became well thought of in that arena, as somebody who could get a show up. And that show actually sold. We did seven episodes for ABC. It was called *Dog and Cat*. It actually introduced Kim Basinger to the world.

LARRY: And from there?

ROBERT: Well, in those days, when you did seven episodes, they actually paid you for thirteen. Then Larry got a TV deal at Paramount. And I had this great office at Paramount, way above my station. If Dan was a college education, Larry was graduate school. I learned more sitting across the desk listening to him talk on the phone. That's priceless. Then NBC offered me a job to be vice president in charge of drama development.

LARRY: So now you were a network executive.

ROBERT: I'd always wondered what went on in those rooms at the network. And I found it was, by and large, whimsy. It was a crazy sixteen months. I saw some really crazy things done. During scheduling season, people would have a shot at going to the board and scheduling.

There had been one show that was on the board for the better part of a week. It was locked into this one time period. And somebody got up and moved some things around, and they took this show and said, "Let's just put it here for the moment." And that thing never got back on the schedule. It had been solid there for four days! Then it got really crazy. Somebody high up got fired. People got fired right and left.

LARRY: Did you take away anything positive from that experience?

ROBERT: I got to meet the second-in-command at Warner Brothers Television. That's where I ended up, with a producing deal.

LARRY: Where did the first real script come from?

ROBERT: My producing partner and I did *V* for television.

LARRY: Neal, did you have a mentor in television?

NEAL BAER: I was very lucky. I had a mentor at *ER* in Paul Manning, who passed away in 2005. He used to spend hours sitting with me, and we would stay up all night. He would be so hard on himself. He would write a script and throw it out.

LARRY: How did he encourage you?

NEAL: When *ER* started, I was a fourth-year med student, a resident through most of the show, and for two years while on *Law & Order: Special Victims Unit*. I would tell Paul about this kid who had come in with some ailment, and I did not look in his ear, and all the doctors yelled at me. And from that, we'd find a story, one that became a big one with Noah Wyle, actually.

LARRY: Gardner, you went to business school. Had writing even crossed your mind?

GARDNER STERN: There was an interest, but I cannot honestly tell you that it was some burning desire inside of me. It was just that when I did a commercial and I heard the words I'd written on the radio, that kind of got me thinking. And then I'd watch TV and think, "This stinks. I could do better!" And that's when I got a copy of a script, and I just wrote one. That's when I started thinking I could do it.

LARRY: Kim, Dallas is a long way from Hollywood. Who inspired you to come out and give it a try?

KIM NEWTON: It was my oldest brother's idea. I had a job as a junior copywriter. I told him I did not like Dallas or advertising. So he, who has always taken risks, said, "Why don't you try being a movie or TV writer? Come out here, live in my guest room, and learn how to be that kind of writer. I have a patient who teaches and used to be a comedy writer." Like Gil Grant, this guy calls me out of the blue, and he wrote for *Get Smart*. I ended up getting this PA job on *Picket Fences* and working my way up the ranks, and then the writers were very helpful to me there and I started writing specs.

LARRY: And that's where we met for the first time. You were an assistant the day I came in to pitch those writers.

KIM: I had to proof all of David Kelley's scripts. I read everything so I'd see it evolve and learned by osmosis.

Chapter 1 Lesson

"I got lucky. I was in the right place, at the right time, discovered by people who believed that I had talent."

That's the answer to the question that began this chapter. So I'm sorry to report that there is no magic bullet for beginning a Hollywood writing career. I don't think I've ever heard of anyone who took exactly the same path as anyone else. As you'll read later, there is no required background or upbringing, there is no need for experience, and no definitive material to write that will attract employers (even great material).

There's a reason. Remember, I asked you to focus on the nature of Hollywood. There is a core concept about it that you must understand: *Everything about Hollywood is arbitrary.* Success is arbitrary. Taste in material is arbitrary. Moving through the hoops to get a project produced contains multiple arbitrary events.

So how can a writer break into Hollywood if everything is based on random occurrences? Before I can answer that question, you must first understand *why* everything is beholden to haphazard events.

A Random Walk Down Hollywood Boulevard

In his landmark book *Hollywood Economics*, Professor Arthur de Vany performed a comprehensive survey of feature-film box-office results over a long period of time, and examined how the results were affected by certain variables. (2003, 11–15).

His conclusion: box-office success cannot be predicted (28–46).

The monetary success of any given movie is arbitrary. Professor de Vany characterized the film business as operating in a field of "extreme uncertainty" (60–62). This point makes sense, because it is impossible to predict how millions of unique individuals will respond to any given unique movie. There are also an infinite number of variables that go into making a movie. Professor de Vany's theory can be extrapolated to television, or to any other medium.

So, success is random.

If success is random, then how can any investor (such as a studio) adequately judge risk and return when the models are extremely uncertain?

They can't. Thus, random success creates a pervasive fear throughout the entire industry. *And that fear controls Hollywood.*

How Other People's Fear Affects the Writer

Imagine these terrified studios with billions of dollars on the line every year. The employees of those studios realize that even just one mistake could cost them their jobs. But they have no secret knowledge to help them through any decision because success is totally random! Woe is them! What are they to do? How do they react?

They become afraid to make decisions.

Because they are more interested in protecting their jobs than producing art, they hire lots and lots of people and create a bureaucracy to slow the process down as much as possible, thereby limiting the number of decisions they will have to make. These people, known in the vernacular as "executives," exist "solely to anticipate and serve the needs of their betters," as David Mamet wrote in his book *Bambi Meets Godzilla* (2007, 82). None of them is operating out of any sense of artistic integrity. They are just interested in keeping their jobs.

(Disclaimer: Some of my friends are executives, and they are actually very nice people who understand how best to support a writer *and* please the studio. But that's for another book.)

So here you come, Writer, all excited to break into television. You are confronted with the following bureaucratic chain preventing you from getting anything original to series (that's you at the bottom):

Corporate owner
Network head
Network executive
Network development staff
Studio head
Studio executive
Studio development staff
Producer
Producer's development staff
Agent
Writer

Too many people, with jobs at risk, must *make a decision* for your script to cross to the next step. Thus, decisions are postponed until each level believes it has done everything possible to protect itself against their superior's criticism or (worse) a flop.

As responsibility for the content becomes greater and greater further up the chain, personnel focuses on how best to insulate oneself from risk, while simultaneously making whatever sacrifice is necessary *to get the TV show made.* They follow these counterproductive courses of action instead of focusing on *what one must do to make the best show possible.*

But What Can I Do about All This?

Now you understand why fear controls Hollywood. But how can you break into Hollywood in the midst of this insanity, where nothing can be controlled, and randomness prevails?

You write. That's something you can control, and you can make your material great. After that point, it's out of your hands, but at least you will be providing Hollywood with what they claim to need.

You can also be prepared, so that when opportunity knocks, you can take advantage of it. Go back and read the interviews again. Notice that everybody was prepared when they were given an opportunity, and if they weren't ready, they faked it by smoking a cigarette.

The best things you can have ready in your arsenal are scripts! The more, the better. You don't need to have a script for every genre, although it obviously increases your chances. In fact, it may be better to do what Jane Espenson did, and specialize in one type of show.

In addition, there is no substitute for life experience. It is critical not just in writing but in television generally. Running shows, for example, is about establishing and respecting the overall creative vision of the show. It requires constant interaction with, and being encouraging of, the creative support staff of the show. A showrunner like Bob Singer needs to know how to talk to people, to encourage them, to inspire them, to reprimand them—all to achieve the goal of putting together a great show. You can achieve that end only through life experience. Bob—he has it in spades.

But life experience isn't just about providing fodder for us to write about or managing groups of people. Life is unfair. Life is challenging and difficult. To survive life, you must be pragmatic. You must compromise. Life's difficulties are magnified working in television. Thus, if you are skilled at managing life, you will be somewhat prepared for managing television.

Life experience also teaches discipline. Gardner and Kim came to writing from other occupations. Gardner was in advertising. Kim was a copywriter. From these arenas, they developed a work ethic. They understood the concept of deadlines. They understood the concept of teamwork.

Now, Gardner and Kim have a job to do: deliver scripts. At the end of the day, the only things Gardner wants from his staff, and the only thing the studio and network want from Gardner, are scripts. The writer who fails to balance idealism with pragmatism does not last very long in a television job.

Further Reading

Mamet, David. 2008. *Bambi Meets Godzilla: On the Nature, Purpose, and Practice of the Movie Business.* New York: Simon and Schuster.

2

How to Be a TV Staff Writer;
or, Why There Is No *I* in *Team*

The following chapter is how finding employment really works in television. It assumes you managed to secure an agent—a process that also has no rules and you can allegedly learn about elsewhere.

Your agent will submit your script to showrunners, studio executives, and network executives. The executives at the latter two entities may eventually read your script from the piles that all the other agencies sent them. They may first read scripts from writers they already know and be biased toward them. They may first read scripts sent by an agent that they know has good taste, that they have a crush on, that they slept with once, or were once married to. They may be offended by what you've written and not give you a chance. They may have once recommended you for a job where you flamed out, so they'll never take a chance on you again. Or perhaps you made them look great, and they'll push you as hard as they can so they can impress the showrunner, eager to earn the showrunner's approval because their self-esteem needs it, because they slept with the showrunner, or because they hope to do so. Maybe they got a ticket on the way to work, stepped on some doggy poop, sat on a tack, lost thousands in the stock market on a "tip" from another writer, or just decide they are going to reject everything they read that day.

Did I mention that Hollywood success is random?

After weeks of reading scripts, some executives may like what you wrote. If they don't know you, they'll set a meeting where any number of other things may bias them for or against you. At the meeting, some want you to be ruthlessly honest about the show they want to recommend you for; others want you to agree with their opinion; others want you to discreetly acknowledge that you know they have the power to hire you. A few executives are just honest people who do their jobs really well, and know how to match a good writer with a show and showrunner.

Eventually, executives create writer lists that run three or four people deep for each show. If, by some miracle, the first writer in line for the job doesn't get it because he wants too much money, or his agent angers the people in Business Affairs, or his agent dumped someone in Business Affairs, or Business Affairs felt pushed around by the agent the last time they struck a deal so they sabotage this first writer's deal, then the other folks get a shot.

If a show is picked up with a veteran showrunner, half the jobs will be filled because he hired his friends, writers he knows he can count on, and a few that got pushed onto him because they have some kind of deal with the studio.

If a show is picked up with a rookie showrunner, he'll have little say over who gets hired because the studios are afraid to let him make those decisions.

Maybe somewhere in here you got the job. Congratulations!

How do you *keep* the job? What are your obligations? What are the rules? How do you maintain the quality of the one thing that got you there in the first place: your writing?

Suggested Viewings

Battlestar Galactica (remake): "The Passage," by Jane Espenson
Law & Order: "Conspiracy," by Rene Balcer and Michael Chernuchin
Homicide: "Three Men and Adena," by Tom Fontana

LARRY: Nobody ever really discusses what it's like to be on the writing staff of a TV show. I'd like to address this topic, so that people can understand the job, the expectations, the political scene, and just how to survive. Javier, you and I worked together on a staff many years ago when we both were starting out. I learned some hard lessons then, and I bet you've learned some along the way.

JAVIER GRILLO-MARXUACH: I'm a supervising producer–level writer, and I'm very handsomely compensated for my efforts. My job is to go in and do it the way they want me to do it. That's the difference between the writer I was on *The Pretender,* which was my second assignment, and the writer I am now. On *Pretender* I still had these feelings of, "I should be allowed to express myself creatively, blah, blah, blah, yadda, yadda." Those pretensions got in the way of what my job was, which was to listen to the executive producers, however much I may have disagreed with what they were doing, and then find a way to put myself into the script. Now, many years and shows later, I know how to adapt to somebody else's working method and put myself into it.

LARRY: Do you find that creatively restrictive?

JAVIER: No, because I just do the mental shift of taking that piece of the creativity and putting it in the Writers' Room instead of into the draft writing. When I'm writing a draft on *Lost,* the outline is so specifically described that I still have to find something in the scene to connect to, obviously. But the creativity becomes making it sing as a script rather than as an outline. Each individual step of it is a work of art in and of itself. Writing a great outline is a different skill set from being able to get stuff out in The Room.

LARRY: Let's talk about The Room for just a moment. This is where the staff convenes to put together the story beats, or scenes. Everybody runs The Room differently. Sometimes there is a clear hierarchy; sometimes there isn't. Sometimes there isn't even a Room at all.

JAVIER: It all depends on how the showrunner has set it up.

LARRY: We'll get into that more, but the important point to understand is this is where the stories are born and nurtured. So, getting back to what you said about each step being creative in its own way—

JAVIER: At this point in my career, the trick that I'm able to mentally say is, "Where am I going to put that aspect of my creativity into the process now?"

LARRY: So as a professional, it's up to you to maximize your creativity and effectiveness, even if the environment is not ideally suited to your process.

JAVIER: Our job is to execute the executive producers' mission. That means we must work the way they want us to work. We must do it the way they want it. Paradoxically, we have to give it to them with our own spark and creativity, or they think we're not doing our job. So the way you reconcile that paradox is that you find a certain creative flexibility within yourself that you're able to move within the elasticity of the material.

LARRY: So there's this nexus, between our voice and their vision, and finding a way to max that out.

JAVIER: There were many shows where I very deliberately copied the executive producers' style because that's the way they liked it. In fact, I was on a show where my first script had been idiosyncratically mine. My script immediately became a "problem script" because somewhere in the executive producer's mind he felt, "Javier just doesn't get it." I was not asked back for the second season. But when I went on to my next show, I very specifically said, "I'm going to write the executive producer's voice," and I did. But it's not a one-way street. If the executive producer is good, and the show evolves and is a hit, I think they open up a bit more and other people's voices are integrated into the show.

LARRY: Melding it with his own vision.

JAVIER: They've heard more of what you have to say and started using it themselves. Your own voice starts coming through, and they begin forgiving you when you start adding variants. Those Darrin Morgan episodes of *X-Files* are the best examples.

LARRY: If the show is evolving, your voice starts creeping into the show because it becomes part of the show's DNA.

JAVIER: I think *Lost* is edging that way. With fourteen leads, everybody brings something to each character that's different and unique. Some of us have brought in stuff for certain characters that stuck. But it's a show that really lends itself to many voices within Damon and J. J. Abrams's greater vision.

LARRY: Can you give me one major creative lesson that you learned from your early shows?

JAVIER: On *Pretender*, I think you and I hit on the perfect episode in "Under the Reds," a combination of the personal emotional moments with the formula. On *Charmed*, that experience was about molding myself to a show, where you have to look at these three actors who were the leads, figure out what they were good at, and write to it.

LARRY: After that you went on to the Sci Fi Channel series *The Chronicle*. I think there may be some writers out there who don't take sci-fi seriously in terms of helping us as writers.

JAVIER: That was one of the single best experiences I had on television. The show's creator, Silvio Horta, was so generous to me. I was able to take the weirdest concepts and marry them to structure and character. I could do a show about Elvis-impersonator vampires.

LARRY: Chris, you worked with Javier on *Boomtown*. He talked about merging a writer's voice with the showrunner's. Is that what's special about whose scripts succeed on a show?

CHRIS BRANCATO: Each script sparkles for the show in its own way. On *North Shore* we had two very different writers. One just could deliver good, solid stories all the time. They all made sense at the end and were emotional. Your lower-level people, generally, turn in something that you pretty much have to do a deep rewrite on.

LARRY: You expect that, though.

CHRIS: But the thing everybody forgets about writing is that it's like baseball. If of the last four scripts, two are good and two aren't, that's a .500 batting average. You know all scripts can't be great. You realize that on your staff you're putting together a mold of personalities, each of whom has a different talent. I want somebody who can do dialogue punch-up. I want somebody who's funny. I want someone whom everybody loves just because they have the personality that enlivens The Room. I want a workhorse to whom I can give four scripts, and they'll get them done.

LARRY: So when you read candidates, what are you pulling out of the stack of scripts and why?

CHRIS: I have a first-level read from somebody in my company, separating the wheat from the chaff. I'm an advocate of sending out spec pilot samples, because they have one's own voice. If it's not brilliant in four pages, then I throw it on the ground.

LARRY: Pretty cut-and-dry.

CHRIS: If you want a six-figure paycheck, you better give me a great script. Then Bert Salke, my producing partner, reads the next wave. We also read people who are suggested to us by agents we know. Then we dwindle it down to a handful of people. I read all those and bring in the best to talk to.

LARRY: Do you feel like the decision has already been made before you meet them?

CHRIS: Oh, no.

LARRY: Because it is about personality.

CHRIS: Yes.

LARRY: What's your feeling about the writers that the studio and network suggest?

CHRIS: We have good relationships with our studios and networks. I haven't had any trouble getting anybody on staff that I wanted to get on staff.

LARRY: We spoke earlier about whether people *like* outlines. Michael, on a show like *Law & Order* you must need outlines because of the mystery elements.

MICHAEL CHERNUCHIN: Yes, and I give more people time to do an outline than a script.

LARRY: And do you subscribe to Javier's theory that there is art in discovering things in the script?

MICHAEL: Yes, the script is the art part of it, not the craft part.

LARRY: I think people might say there isn't room for discovery in *Law & Order*, but I disagree. We meet many characters that appear in just one scene. The great old director Edward Dymytrk once told me that if you've got these one-moment characters, make them come alive, even if they're just the doorman, it adds verisimilitude.

MICHAEL: Absolutely. One of the best lines I ever wrote was a woman's opening line: "The best part about getting old is you only have to do it once." You now know everything you need to know about her. Just the opposite was *Seinfeld*, which they said was about nothing, but was the best-plotted show on TV. And guess what, even *Seinfeld* goes back to Shakespeare. He had these big stories with all these disparate parts that would all come together at the end.

LARRY: Hart, after you left Canada and came here, you started on a show called *Cupid*. Any lessons from that show?

HART HANSON: I was so lucky. Jeff Reno and Ron Osborne came in to help run the show. I was down the chain, so I got a ringside seat to see how editors and directors and actors are treated here. Then there was some political thing that resulted in Reno and Osborne leaving, which meant Rob [Thomas, the showrunner] needed backup, and there I was. I got a crash course in how American network shows are run.

LARRY: So there's a big lesson. Don't just sit and write. Watch, learn, observe. That's part of the job. Was working in America creatively liberating or more restrictive?

HART: Restrictive. In Canada, you get to run the show. If they don't like it, they fire you. Here you get all kinds of input. I learned how to take notes from all these different entities, but had gotten to watch from a distance, so when it happened to me, it was not a shock, and I was able to figure out what my approach would be.

LARRY: Which was?

HART: I'll take any notes that don't matter, which are a huge number. I don't fight them for things that don't matter. So they let me get away with the important stuff because I've given them so much on the other side.

LARRY: So you protect the theme.

HART: The moment that's lost, then I'm lost; I lose everything. I never share what the theme is with the network or studio. I don't think they look at it anyway.

LARRY: And do you use a Room?

HART: No. I think The Room is more about who is the most effective actor as opposed to arguer.

LARRY: Jason, you came from theater. Did you have to reeducate yourself in the storytelling process for TV?

JASON KATIMS: It's very different. With TV writing it's deceptive how different they are.

LARRY: Can you articulate the difference?

JASON: There are many. You get to the story quicker. The kinds of stories you tell are different. Television is similar to film in that much of the storytelling is in the transitions. That's not true in the same way in plays, so much of it is figuring out ways to write the passage of time. I always felt that, for plays, the fewer scene changes you have, the better. The fewer times you cut, the better. It has to be extremely economical. But in television there are several story lines happening continuously.

LARRY: You also have that immediacy with plays that you don't have with television.

JASON: Major factor. Any kind of writing, but particularly in television, you must be brutally honest with yourself. You never get over falling in love with your own writing, your own jokes, and your own cleverness, but that will kill you. What's great about TV is that you get to do twenty-two stories a year, and you're constantly learning by doing. Stuff that seems great on the page may seem redundant in the cut, and that is death. When the audience gets ahead of you, that's death. When you feel like you're being told information as opposed to *really seeing something happening*—all that comes from the script. I always feel humbled sitting in the editing room. Even when episodes generally work, you're your own harshest critic. People are going to watch an episode and say that was great, and I'm always looking at the one story line that I know was bullshit, or I know we never figured out.

LARRY: Let's talk about development. Do you feel like you're able to create something that's really coming from you, or do you still feel pressure from the networks to come up with something that they, at least, perceive as being more "commercial"?

JASON: That's the sixty-four thousand-dollar question. You have to think of the potential disaster that you're going to be living with in five years, so you have to do something that you know you can propel yourself off of. Otherwise, it's drudgery. If you're working on shows that you don't really enjoy, it's a job. You also have to do something that you're going to love but is somehow going to compete with everything else.

LARRY: Is that a function of the networks not knowing what they want?

JASON: Definitely. My job is to not only give them what they want, but something that is specific to me. I think the trap you can fall into in development is the same trap you can fall into on a show: writing with a network in mind. That's a trap because the audience is ultimately what matters. If you're being barraged with notes and thinking, "I've got to write X because I know the network's going to be all over Y," that's a situation you want to avoid at all costs. It is one of the clichés about networks that I find true. They are looking to repeat their recent success, and it's impossible unless you're literally going from *CSI* to *CSI: NY.* So what can you do except give it your best and know that there's no guarantee?

LARRY: That hits on a really important creative point. In film school, they always said, "It's about process, not product." I thought that was ridiculous at first, but now I see they were right. There are so many forces opposing what you really want to do that at a certain point, you have to let the script go. It's going to production; it's going to get changed by the networks; it's going to get changed by the studio. You just have to say, "I told the story I want to tell, and what it becomes after this is what it becomes after this."

JASON: It's tricky because it's an egotistical field that we've chosen, so some ego is necessary. Now, there's a certain amount of arrogance that's a good thing so that you can basically be able to say at a certain point, "This is what it is. Take it or leave it." One of the best stories about that is when Ed Zwick and Marshall Herskovitz created *thirtysomething.* They both were young and very successful, but they had these film careers that they were really more interested in. They did not really care if the show got on. They described that as having a power that they have never had since. So the distinctive shows are usually particular visions from creators who stuck to their guns.

LARRY: Tim, I did a script for you on *Crossing Jordan.* I thought you had a very welcoming staff, which I imagine made the breaking of your difficult stories more bearable.

TIM KRING: Yes. The banes of our existence were these detailed mysteries. Although the show has got strong characters and a loosey-goosey feel, they are still twisty-turny mysteries that are very difficult to break.

LARRY: Do you start at the beginning, or are you at all nonlinear?

TIM: Act 1 always involves your premise, and you have a few obligatory scenes. If we're going to start with X, then somewhere in Act 3 we know *Y* is going to happen. Obligatory moments are just part of the franchise. A body rolls in from the morgue, and somebody done that body wrong, and we need to discover who committed this crime. That sounds like a tiny thing, but it's not small to have that much story. Many shows would kill for that much story.

LARRY: You must throw out so many stories 'cause you get to a point where you can't break the nut.

TIM: That definitely happens, but rather than throw them out, we evolve them into something that works: "I guess this really was not a story about this. It's more a story about her." It gets harder and harder to find the great original ideas, so very few ideas get thrown out on the whole. You don't have the luxury of throwing stuff out and looking for something brand-new. You don't have time.

LARRY: And that's why I've never understood showrunners who toss out entire scripts. You have to make it work.

TIM: That's what I learned in my years of training as a freelancer. I was a rewrite guy. I'm still enough of an optimist that I think you can make anything work.

LARRY: Do you work out the emotional parts within the outlines?

TIM: It's pretty much confined to the plot and story. The emotional parts are discussed in a more amorphous way, and they're the parts that the writers are more interested in, so I don't have to remind them to do it.

LARRY: So you're allowing personal expression?

TIM: Absolutely. None of us are particularly interested in forensic science, so it's a more procedural show. Alan Arkush, our producer-director, has the great analogy that if *CSI* has a scene about a pair of tweezers, then the entire scene becomes *about* the tweezers. On our show, we'll take out a pair of tweezers, and two characters will argue over whose tweezers they are. So every forensic scene actually has this other story going on. We've done lots of episodes in this where we're trying to strike the balance between procedural and character where we've tipped it too far towards the procedural, and ultimately the audience doesn't care when they finish watching it. It always comes back to: "How does the crime affect our characters? How are they changed by it?" And if you're not telling that story, ultimately it's a hollow experience.

LARRY: Do you miss those moments when the show was just starting out? Creatively, I mean.

TIM: We both went to USC film school, and I loved my 290 class, where we made five super-8 movies in one semester. I loved picking up a camera. We did not know what we were doing. The films had this free-spirited quality to them. Then over the course of those three years you unlearn everything! The camera gets locked down, and we start to copy Hollywood film. I always thought that they should have started that curriculum with 290 and then ended it with it again.

LARRY: Come back to where you started.

TIM: I think that that is a great paradigm for being a writer. There's a Zen quality where as a child, you look at Mount Fuji, and it's this unbelievable mountain with majesty and size and grandeur. As you grow older you learn how this mountain was formed and what kind of trees are on it, and you dissect it, and you understand why it's a mountain. It loses all of its majesty and importance. When you transcend that in Zen you learn to experience Mount Fuji as this fabulous thing again. I think that that is the goal in writing, to unlearn all the rigidity and format that you've learned in life. In writing for TV, you find those times when you can come back to writing from pure emotion.

LARRY: *My So-Called Life* leaps to mind.

TIM: I was a huge junky of that show.

LARRY: Winnie Holzman was able to let go of whatever cynicism she had learned as an adult and kept it alive for the show.

TIM: I remember those feelings when I was a teenager. I remember those feelings like they were yesterday. You hope that as a writer you can tap back into that.

LARRY: That's where music helps me.

TIM: Absolutely, because music sends you back to whom you were. You find that you're still that guy after everything you've been through—all the pain and heartache and kids and career and everything—but at the core I'm still this twelve-year-old kid who feels the same exact way. You have to believe what you're feeling. If I'm a regular guy, other people must be feeling the same thing, and that's where you can connect with your audience.

LARRY: You're taking a different approach with your new show, *Heroes.*

TIM: Because there are so many separate stories at the beginning, we can divide them up so that one writer will take this story and another writer will take that story and so on. So, everybody goes off, writes, comes back, and we compile all the work, and then each script is assigned a writer in the rotation—we just go down the rotation—and that writer becomes the writer of record on that episode, and he or she compiles it and takes it from there. Most of them go through me at some point, but what it allows us to do is what we're doing right now: dividing up four scripts, going off with everybody taking a chunk, we all come back, put it together, and suddenly we have four scripts. It allows us to get ahead, and with the way that we're shooting we're taking advantage of the ability to what's called "cross boarding," which means shooting multiple scenes from multiple episodes.

LARRY: Peter, do you prefer breaking stories in a Room with everybody else or on your own?

PETER LENKOV: I like to come in with a pretty bust-out idea; otherwise, you could spend much time talking about life and getting nowhere. If you come in with a fleshed-out concept and a direction for the story, it gets the train moving, and you'll get to the end of the fourth act pretty quickly. I'm very goal oriented. At the end of the day I want to have the story broken, and I won't stop until then. I know everybody has lives, so we want to end at a decent hour.

LARRY: Do you prefer to go to script with a fully fleshed-out outline?

PETER: Yeah, I want to know what's coming, so all they have to do is fill in the dialogue. When you're a staff writer and time is of the essence and you're trying to prove yourself, better go with as much artillery as you can get or as the executive producers will allow you. It's also good for a writer because it teaches the discipline of an outline. The writer can relax and not feel like he's under a microscope.

LARRY: Are younger writers given latitude to come to you with a really off-the-wall idea?

PETER: I would embrace it on a show, but when they are writing a sample script, they're trying to capture the voice of the show. They're trying to follow the rules that are set. They wouldn't want to write that standout different episode, because somebody's going to read it and decide they are not really following the voice. However, if that person ends up on a show, I think they should be bold.

LARRY: So it's not necessary to be the crazy writer with the crazy ideas, but it sure is not a bad thing.

PETER: I think writers just need to capture the show's voice. I haven't yet seen anyone come in and just pitch off-the-wall ideas. I noticed that a Room full of other writers intimidates new writers. You get all these intelligent people sitting in a Room together and to pitch out ideas—it could be embarrassing.

LARRY: Yet that's why they've been hired. A great acting teacher once told me that when you get up in front of those people, you have to remember they want you to be good.

PETER: It's not like you're going in to pitch an idea and everybody's going to laugh at you. But most people just want to toe the party line and not be embarrassed. But I remember starting on *The District* and not knowing these people and pitching a wacky idea. The showrunner was looking at me cross-eyed. But two months later Pam Veasay asked if I was writing that story because they wanted me to do it.

LARRY: Suddenly you were valued for that off-the-wall idea.

PETER: It cemented my place on the show. I started writing all the sweeps shows. So, I think most new writers are afraid to take risks, and they shouldn't be.

LARRY: How did Pam run the show?

PETER: Pam was very accepting, a big believer in being in The Room, and not sitting in her office writing everything. She was, in some ways, better at letting go of certain things, of allowing people to do what they're best at. She did not feel the need to micromanage everything.

LARRY: It helps a show, I think. If the showrunner is not there, you could sit for a week breaking a story that you think is great, and the showrunner might hate it. Boom, you've just wasted a week. Now, do you break stories linearly or jump around?

PETER: Depends. Some come up with a great scene and we'll build a story around it, or it's a great issue, because our show's issue driven.

LARRY: The showrunner rewrites scripts 99 percent of the time in television. Have you ever felt a loss of ownership when that happens?

PETER: I've never had that experience in television. But I've had that experience in film where I lose the Writers Guild arbitration, and it's hell to know that. But you have to remember that you always have that first draft. That's yours. Your voice is the first draft.

LARRY: Yes. Do you still feel pride of ownership when the show's done, your name's on the screen, and you have a product? Is there still fulfillment from that?

PETER: Yeah, even the ones I don't write. If I contribute to a show or help edit it, I still feel good about the contribution. I feel like a proud father.

LARRY: The concept of breaking stories is very interesting. To me, it's science and math. Nonlinear thinking and problem solving were hallmarks of all those college courses I took. Shawn, what's your take?

SHAWN RYAN: They're mathematics. They're equations. A-story plus B-story gives you something different. It's true of editing, also.

LARRY: Some people are just no good at breaking stories but are still great writers. That lends credence to the fact that it may be a function of the training we've had.

SHAWN: One of the ways I supported myself when nobody was hiring me to write was to tutor high school kids for math SATs. I'd go home and write spec scripts, and I think that math seeped into me. I've always been able to look at the board where we'd have several different stories, shuffle them in my head, and tell them in a better way. What's interesting is that the writers are taught to get a job, but you actually have to succeed at many things besides writing.

LARRY: We've talked about a staff writer's job. One of the very first things I was told is my job is to assist my executive producer in carrying out his vision of the show.

SHAWN: I always put it as: "My job was to write the episode and to break the story that the executive producer would write if he had the time to do everything."

LARRY: Javier described that collision between wanting to express one-self and fulfilling the show's vision. Did it bother you in your early jobs about that mandate?

SHAWN: I did feel that, but it did not bother me. I don't know if I got to say what I wanted to say, but I was able to nail the shows and the charac-ters. That's all that matters in some people's books. *Nash Bridges* was a very specific show. We had the "Nash Rules." There was a template set up. Carlton Cuse, the showrunner, would say, "Nash doesn't mess up on the job. The only place he's allowed to mess up is an inability to form a relationship with a stunningly beautiful girl before moving on to the next stunningly beautiful girl." That was his flaw.

LARRY: I'd classify that as restrictive. Didn't that ever get to you?

SHAWN: After three years on the show, yes. That's why I wrote the pilot for *The Shield*. Also, I had a choice to get locked into a fourth year of *Nash*, or move on to *Angel*. The first choice guaranteed me two more years of employment. *Angel* would only guarantee me thirteen epi-sodes, and I knew I'd be proving myself all over again. I chose *Angel* because I'd learned what I could learn on *Nash*. *Angel* was a different show more in line with my sensibilities. I ended up learning much more because of David Greenwalt. So both my attraction to *Angel* and the writing of *The Shield* pilot were in many ways fueled by writing in a narrowly defined zone for three years on *Nash Bridges*. *The Shield* became a pilot where I allowed myself to throw out all the rules.

LARRY: Laurie, you worked on a genre show called *The Kindred*. Genre shows have specific rules.

LAURIE MCCARTHY: In a sci-fi show, you have to establish what the rules are of that world and abide by them.

LARRY: Did you have a Room?

LAURIE: Yes and no. I came onto the show near the end of its order. So many of the writers were either already finished or producing their own episodes. I did, however, inherit an idea someone else had pitched, and believe me, I could have used a Room. The episode was called "Skull." I thought, "Great, creepy, and I get to write it." So I talked to the showrunner, and he said, "Yeah, there's a whole thing for 'Skull' and talk to this other producer about it." But he'd already left the show. So I called him, and he said, "There's a skull." That was it. They find a skull.

LARRY: And, being a pro, off you go.

LAURIE: Off I go, but it was a particularly torturous journey. The writer, who is the greatest, most hysterical guy, by the way, called me for years afterward. I'd pick up the phone, there'd be this silence, and then I'd hear him growl, "Skuuulllll." Click.

LARRY: Excellent. Okay, so you're writing this vampire show. You aren't a vampire as far as I know. So, where is the personal aspect? I ask this knowing the answer, being a genre writer myself, of course, but still . . .

LAURIE: I try to find out what characters are driven by, and what a show is driven by. Many shows you can boil down to one emotion. Maybe you have a show about compromise, about all the horrible compromises that people make with their lives. I thought a show about vampires was really a show about change. So that's where we came from on that show, and there were good vampires and bad vampires. It was a mafia show. There were tribes always at war with each other.

LARRY: What did you learn from shows where there was a Room?

LAURIE: I learned how to really work my Room from John Eisendrath on *90210*. That was a Room every day, all day.

LARRY: Wow. See, my take is a bit like Peter's. Unless you're dealing with a mystery show, you have no excuse to be breaking story for days on end. That happened on many shows I've been on. It drives me nuts. An environment where you're all there in one room—it's just psychically taxing.

LAURIE: Let me clarify. Sometimes you'd leave The Room, but you had other writers who stayed. You're in there part of the day a couple of days a week. You don't need to be in there all of the time. I also don't think you all have to be in there.

LARRY: I do find The Room very helpful in breaking logjams or just coming up with ideas.

LAURIE: I'm used to thinking aloud. But I find that if there's no structure in The Room, it can get unhealthy. I think it's good to have a couple days a week where everybody is there. People, especially in the beginning of a series, help form the series as a whole. I do think that when there's no Room, people get left out.

LARRY: Is breaking story simply a structural exercise for you? Do you go totally linear?

LAURIE: No, but I never forget that there's a structure. I *almost* never forget. But there's more about The Room that's good, better than pitching over the phone, particularly if you're the one who's vetting The Room ideas, including your own. And that's being able to look in the staff writer's face. You know they're not going to say that your idea sucks, but I can tell when it sucks. You can kind of tell when it comes out of your mouth.

LARRY: It takes on a life of its own when you pitch it back out to someone, doesn't it? It's like, you've heard it, and it really did suck. What did you take away from *90210*?

LAURIE: I learned how to write an ensemble show, interweaving four or five story lines. I also learned to keep scenes short, because a page and a half is almost long enough for anything. In television, you want to switch the theme before they want to switch the channel.

LARRY: How do you run a Room?

LAURIE: With as much encouragement as possible. It's hard because I'm limited by deadlines and potential obstacles and my own sense that I am free-falling into the abyss. Meaning, we have to finish this episode and then move on to the next, and every extra day this one takes is a day lost on the next. So it's always a struggle between moving forward and giving each episode and idea the time it deserves. Having said all of that, you also need to have fun. I've worked with the greatest writers the last couple of years, and I want to know what they think about everything. I want to know what they think about the elections, what movie they saw—everything. And you need to do that, just park your work brain and enjoy your colleagues every once in a while.

LARRY: Frank, when you were writing that *Miami Vice* script, would you say you were working instinctually? Or did you feel you had to slave over every word?

FRANK MILITARY: No, it was instinctual. I did not even watch television, so I did not even understand *Vice*. I had the expectation it was going to be a onetime thing anyway, so it did not really matter. They clearly made a huge mistake, and they'll suss it out and I'll be fired.

LARRY: And then on the second script was it the same thing?

FRANK: Yeah. I kind of just plowed ahead with it, and that one did not go until I got more notes, and that was kind of frustrating. I did not realize that that would be the rest of my life, getting notes. I just kind of plowed ahead with it and the same thing when I did *The Equalizer*.

LARRY: Bob, do you prefer to have detailed outlines, either for yourself or from your staff? Or are you more comfortable with having just beats?

ROBERT SINGER: What I do is not fair, because when I'm doing it I only use signposts. The first thing I do for hour television is come up with act ends. Those are the relay targets you have to hit. Then I write notes of what I want from the characters—what they will go through and what the character arcs are. Because although I know the good story is really everything, I want the story to support the characters, not the other way around. I'm just not that clever a plot writer that somebody's going to be wowed by my plot. Then I'll just write beats. But even then, as I write the script, surprises happen. So although the skeleton of it remains the same, much of the flesh becomes different.

LARRY: I've worked both ways. I've been asked to do really detailed outlines; I've been asked to just do beats. I find I can work either way, but I find when I do outlines that are too detailed that it takes some of the discovery out of the writing for me. Whereas having a looser body, if I know where I'm going emotionally, as well as what the story needs to do, I find that if I'm making these discoveries as I write, there's just more snap to the material.

ROBERT: I can't argue that. I don't think there's a right or wrong. I think it's what works for that writer. My wife, who is a wonderful writer, does incredibly detailed outlines. Then she writes scripts so fast that it spins your head. For her, the major part of the work goes into getting the story line. For me, it's the other way around. I remember the *Reasonable Doubts* pilot. I got towards the end of Act 2, and I killed the character that was supposed to be very instrumental to the story in Act 4. And I just went with it. I thought, "Jeezo, you're gonna write yourself into this terrible box." But then I wrote myself out of it, and it turned out really cool.

LARRY: Do you use a Room?

ROBERT: Not really. We do big Rooms to get the big picture on things a few times a year. I'll have writers with mini-Rooms to do script critiques. It's an uncomfortable place, but at least they get it all at once, and coming out we can reach a consensus.

LARRY: Do you find people are sometimes trying to give notes to impress?

ROBERT: I don't think so. I got a really great bullshit meter.

LARRY: Kim, do you prefer a brief outline or a longer one?

KIM NEWTON: I like a longer one for me. I've been on shows like *X-Files* where you just do cards, there is no outline, and you pitch on the phone to the executive.

GARDNER STERN: The studio or network had to approve the story on Chris Carter's show? I'd have thought he could get away with saying, "I'm going to do it whether you like it or not."

KIM: His whole thing was, "I'm teaching you how to be writer-producers so you sell your story to the network. Call them up, say Chris has approved this and that I just wanted to tell you the story." You had to do everything regardless of what level you were at. It was actually a really good place to start. You were thrown to the wall, you were on your own, there was no help, and everybody was competitive and hoped you fail. That aspect of it was not pleasant, but it was like going to Vietnam and coming back. Everything now is easy in comparison.

LARRY: So you like to have a longer outline for yourself?

KIM: Yes. I still like to be able to have the freedom. I just feel a little more secure when I start writing. I know what my map is. *Las Vegas* is a little easier in those respects. We do short outlines with A-, B-, and C-stories, we break them separately, then use them in outline form mixed together.

LARRY: That's actually how I was taught. Now, being able to produce your own episode, and therefore have even more creative input, at the end do you feel this is your episode? What if the story you set out to tell has been changed?

KIM: Over time you've got to let go of that. That happens early in your career where you think the whole thing is ruined when your favorite line of dialogue gets cut. You're just going to torture yourself and make yourself miserable because the reality of television is that if it's not your show, the episode is never going to be exactly what you want it to be.

LARRY: Writing is also a learning process. In all the shows, all the episodes that you've done, do you still feel like you're learning something every time?

KIM: I think I learn something each time I write something new, at least in some small way, because every story is different. I get less nervous about working, too. I'm used to changing jobs, and I don't really get nervous about writing a first draft on a new show anymore. I'm going to write the way I write and see how it goes.

LARRY: I imagine much of it has to do with the tone that your showrunners set up?

KIM: It's about being comfortable with your writing style. They hired you, saw your writing style, and so the trick is not to write out of fear. Some people write well out of fear, but I do not. If you start to wonder, "Do they really want me here?" you sabotage yourself. When I did *X-Files*, Chris Carter offered me the job because this writing team had left and *they* had offered me a job on their new show. He wanted me desperately because he wanted to screw *them*. But I knew that, it really bothered me, and that writing team really wanted me because I was *me*. Chris wanted me because it was about *them*. So you just have to trust yourself, and I think that comes with time.

Chapter 2 Lesson

Episodic television has a schedule that is somewhat leisurely enough for debate over story and script. Oftentimes, that debate takes place in The Room.

You need to know more than just how to behave in The Room. You need to know why to behave in a certain way.

The Room

The Room is a large conference space, often supplemented with various foodstuffs that are high in carbohydrates. It is usually windowless. Your fellow writers will often fight over the thermostat. I happen to like the room to be freezing, but most of my colleagues prefer it to be much warmer.

You will discover various archetypes exist in The Room. Every one of them has a place in The Room. Every one is needed in some way at some time (except for one). There is The Whiner, who perpetually complains about the network's and studio's terrible script notes. There is The Logic Nazi, who ferrets out every logical hole in a story. There is The Pleaser, who always tries to impress the most senior producer in The Room at the moment. There is The Socialite, who somehow knows virtually everyone in television. There is The World Traveler, who regales the group with tales of strange adventures in far-flung, exotic locales that he or she swears are all true (this includes claiming to have once smoked crack with Ted Kennedy). There is Structure Dude (or Dudette), who is able to place all of the scenes in just the right order, no matter how unconnected they may seem. There's Professor Idea, an idea machine who constantly thinks up ideas for a beat or a scene or a show concept. There's the Idea Assassin, who always finds a reason for an idea not to work. An Idea Assassin usually gets fired (that's the one you don't need). There's The Politician, who is keenly aware that an unhappy show often creates political scenarios that must be navigated to save jobs.

Then there's you, The Rookie. How do you behave, and why? Here are my Eight Commandments of The Room for new writers:

1. Thou Shall Be Thyself. If you survive on the show, it will be far too much work to have to act all the time. Just be you. If the people you work with are decent folks, they'll like you. If they're demons, they'll find a reason to dislike you and you'll want a new job anyway.

2. Thou Shall Do No Harm. Do not be an Idea Assassin. If you see a reason an idea won't work, let someone else find it, until you've been on the show for several weeks and your story sense can be trusted.

3. Thou Shall Be Professor Idea. Even bad ideas can spark good ideas. Be prudent at first—you want to offer ideas when The Room is confounded with a problem.

4. Thou Shall Know Thy Place. Every show is political. There's much you won't know when you first arrive. Tend to your knitting. Do your work.

5. Thou Shall Work Hard. You are being assessed. Arrive a half hour before anyone else does each day, and leave after everyone else (except the showrunner).

6. Thou Shall Be Involved. To the extent that you are permitted to do so, be as involved in producing your episode as you can. There's much to learn.

7. Thou Shall Get to Know the Crew. Get to know everybody on set, when time permits. They are there to make your show great. Ask them about what they do. People love to talk about their craft. They'll like you for asking, and you'll learn much.

8. Thou Shall Support Thy Showrunner. It's the showrunner's show and career on the line. Be a good soldier.

The "why" behind these "how-to" rules is survival. None of these rules has to do with writing. Every workplace has a hierarchy and politics. You need to be aware of them and respect them. If you don't, even an Emmy Award won't save you.

What Goes Down in The Room

While snacking, and drinking endless cups of coffee, you and the other staff writers "break story." Scene ideas are tossed around. Character objectives and attitudes are debated. Just as a sculptor molds a masterpiece from clay, the writing staff builds their product from ideas—the more, the better. Many times the most innocuous comment may change the entire story. Entire story arcs can be shot down in seconds, trashing days of hard work. The Room is fickle.

Ideally, The Room also is where a writer's vanity and possessiveness must fall away. The staff is there to carry out the showrunner's vision, and ultimately, the showrunner is the final arbiter. Any writer who attempts to usurp the process may become ostracized by others, or at the very least resented. Nobody likes a showboat. Nobody like a kiss ass. Sometimes the dynamics of The Room are skewed toward impressing the showrunner. These shows tend to have poor working environments as a whole. Sometimes the dynamics of The Room are skewed toward making a great series. These shows tend to have great working environments.

The story being discussed in The Room will usually be written by one of the staff in outline form, and then expanded into a script. This person will likely want to be able to emotionally connect with some part of the material. The best staffs are able to recognize what elements the writer desires and, within given time constraints, assist the writer in formulating a story that plays toward the chosen theme. At the same time, however, the writer must also be flexible. Sometimes an idea arises that is of greater value to the series as a whole than to the individual episode. Should that happen, the writer must find something else to hang onto emotionally.

The Room is the writing staff's inner sanctum. In many ways, it is considered a creatively holier place than the writer's own desk. The Room requires unexpurgated commentary. It should be as safe a place for writers as workshops are for actors. Self-censorship hurts the show and harms the team. What may appear to be a terrible idea at first may later return to save the entire episode. As such, the best shows have Rooms where writers can and do share their personal experiences—even the most shocking or embarrassing or humorous ones.

These moments are truths laid out in their barest form, and as we will learn, truth is what audiences and writers ultimately seek. This sharing of life experience also bonds the staff. It's good for everyone.

The worst type of Room is where ideas are mocked, creativity is squashed, and insensitive and arrogant producers crush morale. Some showrunners and their lieutenants let success go to their heads. Knowing the writers are fearful of losing a plum job, they make life difficult for their compatriots. Some showrunners feel so pressured that their first level of attack is on their own people. Insulting or degrading remarks always have the opposite effect than what is intended. Writers who do not feel valued tend to shut down. They withdraw. As a result, the flow of ideas grinds to a halt. The showrunner has hastened his own demise.

Further Reading

Marcus Aurelius. 2000. *Meditations.* New York: Vintage.
Maxwell, John C. 2002. *The 17 Essential Qualities of a Team Player.* New York: Thomas Nelson.

3

How to Make Your Writing Personal; or, Why You Must Take the "Me" Out of It

Once the writer begins to write, an ephemeral process begins. It involves the mind, the heart, memory, logic, and, most of all, a desire to find the truth. At least, that's what most writers hope to achieve. However, by the time you've landed on a television show, you're just happy to have put out a script that is entertaining and perhaps meaningful in some tiny way.

Nevertheless, for audiences to buy into your stories, your characters must feel real. They must behave in emotionally honest ways. Audiences know when they're witnessing something false. So if the material isn't directly drawing from some personal experience, it had better at least feel universal.

This point brings us to several intertwined questions because they deal with a complex process that is difficult to define. It's time to ask what specific material can be drawn from actual personal experience, how it can best be conveyed, whether to fear the expression of truly personally powerful moments, and whether writing something "personal" is even a good idea when writing for television.

This chapter will start to get to the heart of the most important "why": why do you want to write?

Suggested Viewings

Crossing Jordan: "Miracles & Wonders," by Tim Kring
The Pretender: "Under the Reds," by Javier Grillo-Marxuach and Lawrence Meyers
Deadwood: "Pilot," by David Milch

LARRY: Michael, is your work coming from a place of personal emotional experience?

MICHAEL CHERNUCHIN: The first thing every writer writes about, since Shakespeare's time, is themselves. It's unavoidable. You don't know anything about the world. You look at Fitzgerald's first book, and it was about Princeton. Hemingway was always about himself. But then something happens in life, you grow up and become mature, and you see the universality in what you're feeling, and that's when you're on to something.

LARRY: How long did that take for you?

MICHAEL: Once I started in Hollywood. Much of the stuff I used to do was too personal. It was too much about me. And you have to take the "me" out of it.

LARRY: And yet the "me" is something necessary, even intrinsic, to developing a voice.

MICHAEL: There's a fine distinction. By "me," you have to depersonalize the experience, and make it universal. That doesn't exclude developing the voice, which is the method by which you deliver the story.

LARRY: And by universal, you refer to fundamental human truths that are recognizable to everyone?

MICHAEL: Yes, and to try and do it in a fresh way, to do something where nothing was before. I also realized that if you're writing something totally off the wall, and if it interests you, then it's bound to interest someone else out there because of the universality of the human experience.

LARRY: But if it is off the wall, don't you risk alienating the audience?

MICHAEL: There's an audience for everything. I ask, "Who is that someone I'm writing for?" The answer came after I got out of graduate school and once talked to Kurt Vonnegut. He told me something I keep in the back of my mind. Whenever he's writing, he writes for one particular person. That person can change from page to page, chapter to chapter, book to book. But if you make that one person laugh, somebody in the audience will laugh; if you make that person cry, somebody will cry. So you've got to have an audience in your mind. And it

works. It was amazing when I introduced a character on *Law & Order*.
Many people thought he was someone from my own experience, but
in fact it's because they recognize something about that character that
they know to be true.

LARRY: Michael makes a really intriguing point about taking the "me"
out of it. Although keeping it personal in the most literal sense can
produce rewards, it's also scary. Writers face this fear of revealing
whom we are and what is emotionally going on with us. How do you
get around that, Vanessa?

VANESSA TAYLOR: Many writers have that fear of the blank page. They
feel upset when they're writing. They have dread. I don't know if it's
fear of revealing. I have always thought it was sort of fear of failure. "I
have this thing I want to express. What if I can't?"

LARRY: So this is where that discipline comes in.

VANESSA: It's all about words on the page. If I start writing and it's
terrible, or not what I intend, I'll just keep writing. I don't think I
have fear of revealing myself in that way. Some of my stuff has been
pretty raw. The story that I wrote for Russell Banks in a writing class
was so bizarre in its tone and dialect, and very sexual. I think with
that story, I was fearful of what I was expressing, and of what the
response would be. I just thought it was kind of gross. But it wasn't,
maybe because of Russell and that class.

LARRY: Was the response positive?

VANESSA: The response was incredibly positive and much more positive
than the response to safer material.

LARRY: Why, do you think?

VANESSA: Because it was vastly more interesting. There are times when
you're writing, and you don't remember what you've written, because
you're just spaced out. And that whole story was that way. I did not
know where it had come from.

LARRY: I believe audiences have radar for truth. I bet that's the reason
they responded positively. Carol, do you bring something personal to
your scripts?

CAROL BARBEE: Always. You must bring something that is important to
you. But you also have to be aware that the nature of television is that

the story will likely morph during the process, and you may lose your original intent.

LARRY: When that happens, and you suddenly find yourself unable to relate personally to the material, what do you do?

CAROL: That happened to me once on *Providence*. I was doing a very complex story, and somewhere along the line I lost my way. Bob DeLaurentiis took it over to do a pass, and it was a huge relief! So in that case, I kind of escaped having to face what a mess I'd made of it! Normally, however, you just need to be aware that if your story gets lost, doors to other stories open, and you just need to stay on top of it to see where they lead. Hopefully, they lead to something personal.

LARRY: Hart, when you're writing on someone else's show, even if the show isn't initially personal for you, do you find a way to make it personal, or on an issue show can you grind your axes?

HART HANSON: Oh, yeah. On *Judging Amy*, I became invested in things. I did research into the juvenile justice system and became outraged at what happens to children in this country. Education is a disaster. Foster care is a meat market. Child porn. Bad parenting. And attacking all that can be very satisfying.

LARRY: Chris, how did you discover personal connections to your material?

CHRIS BRANCATO: It's part of you. What you try and do is find a theme in whatever kind of script you're writing that's really interesting to you, separate and apart from creating the story. It's hard to do when you're writing a *North Shore*. It's easier to do when you're doing a *Boomtown*. I do prework brainstorming that's not tied to the tract of the narrative, trying to define the characters.

LARRY: Separate from making the linkage of scenes make logical sense?

CHRIS: Right. When you're forming a narrative you create one scene after another to make sure it all makes sense. I sit for hours and ponder scene possibilities, picture the characters taking one viewpoint and then with the points reversed. I'll examine what effect that has, and I write down what those things are. So I'll come up with a hundred and fifty different scenes, even though the teleplay will only have thirty. So I choose the ones that really feel dynamic.

LARRY: Is that an emotional process, or is it strictly intellectual?

CHRIS: It's pretty intellectual, I must say. The emotional part comes in on a couple of levels. It comes in the moment when I'm done writing dialogue and when I understand what the theme is. Then I can try to get heated with my characters, go back and sculpt it, but retain the essence of the way people's emotions really should play.

LARRY: Do you find taking breaks helps with that?

CHRIS: Yes, you get a sense of where it's lacking in emotion or if it's overdone. Then you rewrite it and let people read it. That's the only way you can really know whether it's affecting people emotionally. But it's an interesting mix of imagination and creative process. I'm half German, half Italian, but the German part of me makes me great with structure. The Italian part is dialogue.

LARRY: Javier, does personal expression come into your work?

JAVIER GRILLO-MARXUACH: Well, I've written stuff about things that preoccupy me politically.

LARRY: Politics often makes people very emotional. It also seems that political opinion is driven by emotion.

JAVIER: That's true. So in that sense, yes. I can't help but write about things that are personally important. However, as a writer who's done mostly genre stuff, I'm always writing about myself but finding allegorical and metaphorical ways to disguise it.

LARRY: Thus, taking the "me" out of it.

JAVIER: Exactly.

LARRY: Now, separate the issue between writing something personal versus writing something emotional.

JAVIER: It all comes out anyway. You're writing about what hurts you, what offends you, what upsets you. That's really it. It was not until I started writing in television that I specifically looked at myself and said, "My gosh, I really have to get better at writing emotional scenes between characters." Because, for example, on a show like *The Pretender*, every week we had to bring in a new set of characters that Jarod cared about. So we had to write some tragic backstory. I always felt like that was my weakest part of the writing. In fact, that one episode you and I cowrote ["Under the Reds", Season 1] worked great because you handled that more emotional stuff.

LARRY: But at the same time, it wouldn't have worked without you setting the stage with the story points.

JAVIER: My strongest suit had always been the pure invention part of writing. That was the downside of writing for escape rather than writing for personal realization. I think the breakthrough for me was when I wrote a play in college. It was a very typical narrative for a young writer, about a screenwriter in the 1930s who gets stuck in a movie serial and how he'd escape. It was about his issues with the characters that he created, and I don't want to overanalyze this fun piece, but the interesting thing was it really was about how unfair the stereotypes of the characters were to the characters themselves. I can look at that and say it's all very clearly about escape. It was about being dissatisfied about where I was in life. It was about having emotions and feelings that were not being serviced by the frame into which I was put.

LARRY: So the things that were important to you were emerging dramatically, and almost organically.

JAVIER: Yeah, but I never set out to write that.

LARRY: That's probably the best way. What you just described is subtext, really. I suppose that if one is going to do something personal, best to leave it to the subconscious and to the subtext, rather than be in your face about it.

JAVIER: Otherwise, you risk ending up with those awful teen "coming-of-age" movies that everyone in film school made.

LARRY: And yet, if done right, those coming-of-age stories can be fantastic. Witness *My So-Called Life*. Jason, how did you handle Angela in that show?

JASON KATIMS: The thing that was difficult about writing Angela was not so much whether I could relate to her, because her experiences were universal, but that her voice-over was so specific as Winnie Holzman's creation. It is Winnie's voice, the method by which her story was delivered, that elevated it beyond what that genre can too easily become.

LARRY: And as a staff writer, the best you can do is approximate that voice based on what you know from your own experience.

JASON: Yeah. But I find that when I'm writing characters that somebody else created, I write them as if they were my own creation. Obviously, you do that within a context of being consistent with whom they are. But because the showrunner is going to do a rewrite, and presumably you've been hired because you understand the characters, then you do the best you can within those parameters.

LARRY: Are you able to directly translate experiences, emotion, and things about yourself into writing?

JASON: I think that's always what you're doing when you're writing. It is a way of using your own experiences, of your friends and loved ones, as raw material to construct stories. Writing is like acting, in that you're trying to find a way to find yourself in the character. You need to find a way in the story. In television, sometimes you are assigned stories. You have to enliven a story that you may not personally connect to. The best method for me is to gravitate towards certain characters. When I came onto *Boston Public*, I loved Michael Rapaport, I'd worked with him before, and he was on the show. I thought there was more to do with him, so I immediately started writing toward that character.

LARRY: In talking about the emotional stuff you need to bring to a script, I break it down into two categories. There's a thin line between them. There's the emotionality of something that you can *relate* to versus a thing that is really and truly deeply felt. I became a father a few years ago. Now all of a sudden, things with kids, I *feel* it. Tim, are you able to write the things that you can *relate* to, or must it be that you *know* it from the inside?

TIM KRING: Over twenty-two episodes you have to have both muscles flexing. If you're lucky, it's something you really are connected to. For me, it's finding some character's point of view, where it can be really rewarding to impart my sense of wisdom or humor or questions about the world. It can be really rewarding to have a character say those things out loud and explore the responses. I've done lots of stories that have a quest for personal meaning in life. I think my best writing was early in *Crossing Jordan* when I had the luxury of thinking about what I wanted to do next.

LARRY: No time for that now.

TIM: No way. I'm on a train, and if I get lucky I can throw a tiny little moment into the script. My best work reflected something that I was going through, like fatherhood or a parent dying. I was able to find moments and entire stories that dealt with things that I was going through in my life and exorcise them by having somebody else deal with them.

LARRY: Now we're starting to veer into Joseph Campbell territory, trying to find meaning in writing.

TIM: Here's a perfect example. I hit and killed a deer one night driving down Beachwood Canyon and had a real strange reaction to it. One was sort of the apocalyptic nature that this deer—a wild animal— was in an urban neighborhood a block away from Gelson's Market. I literally stuck it into a story in *Downtown Boston*. I tried to save the deer's life, and ultimately the deer resurrects and comes back to my life. I was able to exorcise the guilt and those feelings about this animal. That's kind of the beauty of it.

LARRY: It took me a while to figure it out, but that's certainly what I'm doing in writing. I wanted to write an *NYPD Blue* spec. I was trying to come up with an idea while walking down the street one day. These four kids in a Corvette drove up and said, "Are you Jewish?" I thought, "Oh, no. There is no good answer to that question." I turned around and walked the other way, they came back again and asked me again, and I said, "No." I felt so awful denying that part of myself, even though it may very well have saved my life. So I put this whole thing into an *NYPD Blue* script where they asked this old Jewish man, and he said, "Yes," allowing that part of me to answer the way I wanted to. Now, in my script, they shoot him and he dies. So it became about the price of standing up for oneself. And guess what? That script got me so much work because people saw the honesty of it.

TIM: I'd love to say that I'm able to do that. On a TV show you're constantly dealing with actor problems, and production problems, or just shifting landscape of what the network wants. It becomes harder and harder to tap into connecting your own life. You're literally just trying to plug holes.

LARRY: Shawn, tell us what moved you to write *The Shield.*

SHAWN RYAN: I talk much about how the show is different from me. The character of Vic Mackey is very confrontational. That world is full of fighting and unspeakably horrible crimes, and I'm not into that world at all. So the easy answer is it came from my imagination. But obviously there's something in me that's into that perverse kind of thing.

LARRY: Ah, perhaps Carl Jung's concept of the Shadow works within you!

SHAWN: It may! After the first season, when people met me for the first time, they would comment that they expected me to be a lot different.

LARRY: You have many different perspectives represented in the show, ethnic and otherwise.

SHAWN: My childhood was in a midwestern city, and I went to college in this very small town in very white Vermont. Many different ethnicities play soccer. I'd play with Hispanic kids and Caribbean kids. In high school, I was with an all-star team that traveled through Europe. So when I came out here I was very affected by the multiethnicity of Los Angeles. I took a bus to work at the law firm, and being the minority was really interesting. I was out here for the riots, the Northridge earthquake, O. J. Simpson, and the Rampart scandal. When it broke I was writing the script, but what it lacked was this dirty-cop Rampart-esque angle.

LARRY: I'm trying to hunt for the fascination that you must have had for these characters that they came from your imagination.

SHAWN: This is where I think the athletics comes in because I view the Strike Team in the same way that athletes deal with each other. Most male writers come from very studious backgrounds, and there is an alpha-male attitude in the world of sports that I think extends to firemen, to cops, and to military people. There's this small culture out there that I actually think was underrepresented on Hollywood type-writers. I think some people try to fake it. My view of how the world is isn't Pollyannaish. As a well-meaning liberal I believe that one's sexuality shouldn't have anything to do with whether one could make a good cop, but I know that's not how it really is. One of the things in the first season was I wanted to show a gay cop and not show the Hollywood version of that.

LARRY: Did you do any research?

SHAWN: The *L.A. Times,* and the Rampart scandal, was the research.

LARRY: Did you classify Vic as being the guy you wanted to be on the soccer field? It seems almost the direct opposite in many ways.

SHAWN: I did not always feel confident off the soccer field.

LARRY: He's kind of an iconic male figure in many ways.

SHAWN: I still don't know exactly how to define him. There are contradictions with him. It's always a gut feel for me to see the scene, how he should behave and what he should do.

LARRY: Peter, when you bring an idea to the table, do you feel you have a certain luxury of being able to find a story that you can make personal in some way?

PETER LENKOV: When I first started on *The District,* the showrunner said to me, "You're the wrong choice for this show. That's what makes you so right for it, because you're not thinking like we're thinking. You're thinking a little differently. And you're going to make the show that much more special or add something to it rather than just get somebody that's going to just do what I do." And every episode I did was outside the box for them.

LARRY: So maybe not anything personal per se, but personal in your sensibility.

PETER: I want to add some value, like an executive adds value to a corporation so the stockholders feel comfortable and they want to invest in that company. I want people to invest in the show. I want people to watch the show, I want people to know the show, and I want to add something to it.

LARRY: Laurie, were you able to draw on personal experience and emotion while doing those soaps?

LAURIE MCCARTHY: Oh, God, yes. I'd have a fight with my husband, and it would show up in the script the next day. Or I'd write a fight in the script and then find myself having it with my husband the next day.

LARRY: So you really had art imitating life.

LAURIE: And life imitating TV.

LARRY: As you've moved on to other jobs, did you feel spoiled that you could creatively bring so much of yourself to that but maybe not to another show?

LAURIE: No. Because at some point you want to tell stories that are bigger than yourself. The stuff that I wrote for daytime was relatively down-to-earth. Straight up relationship stories, for the most part. The other thing I don't miss is the volume of work. With soaps, you're shooting five episodes a week.

LARRY: Have there been situations where you need a script, don't have time, and decide to just go totally on craft, without adding anything personal to it?

LAURIE: No. I can't speak for other people, but you always have something of yourself in it, whether it's out of your ego or your limited perspective or your intent to make it something people care about.

LARRY: Gardner, any need for something personal in your work?

GARDNER STERN: Not necessarily. If you're a good writer, you can write whatever needs to be written by just relying on craft. It helps much if you're writing a story that you have some personal connection to or can draw upon a personal experience for. Also, you can by proxy relay the personal experience of a friend or a relative. What separates good writers from bad ones is that they can take that foundation and build upon it by just writing dialogue that sounds like the way people really speak. I have not led an unusually dramatic life, but everybody can relate to certain experiences and extrapolate. I'd have to say that specific recollections do not commonly find their way into my writing.

LARRY: You were on *NYPD Blue* for a while. Did you ever find yourself emotionally hooked into a real story because of its circumstances?

GARDNER: No. What I would find myself hooked into was a great story, and being proud to write it and make it come out great.

LARRY: Did you have an affinity for a particular character?

GARDNER: Well, I wrote the character Sipowicz, and I think many people related to him. He was the most complex character, and the actor was a great guy. Some of the best stuff I wrote for that show involved him and not necessarily the cop stuff.

LARRY: So emotional connection isn't really required. As Michael said initially, it's just that human beings are able to empathize.

GARDNER: For example, writing a scene about a first date is something anybody can relate to. Just take those characters, and decide what they will do. I know what I did when I was on first dates. So in that sense I mine my own experience. But on *NYPD Blue,* where I wrote this scene where Fancy takes Sipowicz to a black rib joint, I'd never experienced anything like that. Although, now as I reflect, that might have come out of a similar experience.

LARRY: Which was?

GARDNER: I remember going with my grandfather to play golf, tagging along with him and being in this shitty locker room, learning that was the caddie's locker room because they did not allow Jews to use the real locker room. So the extent of prejudice, maybe there's something there.

KIM NEWTON: I think any good writer just recognizes a good story, period. But I think my first instinct is to go to what I know. I'm not sure I'm even conscious of it in the moment, but when I look back over my body of work I see themes. It's because there's a kernel of something that I can relate to it. There are things you're just attracted to, for whatever the reason is.

LARRY: I think most writers would agree that intellectualizing what those things are might actually harm the creative process. Then you become aware of it, and either steer away from it or try to only find things that fit that paradigm. I think the lesson here is that emotional connections aren't required to write a good story, but to the extent that they reflect universal human truths, then the better off you are likely to be. Who wants to write something that nobody can relate to?

Chapter 3 Lesson

Back to our central question: why do you want to write? Here is one possible answer: you are seeking truth.

Artists and audiences both seek it. Audiences may not realize that is what they seek, as they talk about their yearning for "escapist entertainment," but truth is what they hunger for. Writers may not even realize that is what they seek, but they know when a scene feels "right." Generally, it's because they've found the truth to a scene.

Everyone has a different process for finding it on the page, but ultimately our writers seem to tell us that they first must find the truth within before they can put it on the page. That may be the scariest thing about writing.

But what does "truth" really mean when it comes to drama? Calling a scene "honest" or "accurately reflective of life" is vague. It doesn't really explain why certain pieces of drama can have such tremendous resonance for viewers. Saying that a work is "personal" doesn't cut it, either, because a personal work may not be truthful and a truthful work may not be personal.

We have to go way beyond these petty descriptive words to get at what audiences are looking for when they watch television, and what writers should be aiming for when they compose. As we do, however, remember that some of the process that we are about to learn occurs in our unconscious. What we need to do is learn how to bring it to our conscious mind to help us tell a story.

Fanciful Associations

I'm going to turn to writer-producer David Milch who, in his lecture series titled "The Idea of the Writer" (2007), discusses the concept of "fanciful associations." The best example of a fanciful association is when you hear a particular song that conjures up some kind of memory for you. The association you make between the song and that memory is a purely personal one, but that song will not have that same association to anyone else. It's personal and unique to you, and thus defined as *fanciful*.

Now, if you attempt to dramatize the song with your specific associative moment in a show, it will have very little impact. Somehow, as Michael Chernuchin said, "You have to depersonalize the experience, and make it universal." In Milch's words, how do you make that fanciful association into an "imaginative association," where a commonality of experience that is accessible to everyone's imagination will give that moment resonance? He says that you must "neutralize what is initially fanciful and find the common association."

How does a writer do that? You must drill down deep into your psyche. You must "rest transparently in the spirit which gives you rise." You must be in what I call "The Zone."

As an example, I'm going to use a pathetically weepy and adolescent fanciful association because of the power it has for me. Let's see if I can make it universal.

It's 1983, and one of the eternally replayed songs on the radio is Genesis's "That's All." Simultaneous to the release of this song on the airwaves, I was utterly smitten with a girl named Christine in my high school. Shoulder-length straight brown hair, slight cute overbite, pretty smile. Frequently wore a denim jacket whose sleeves hung just below her hands when she strolled with her arms at her side. We had some interaction, as we had a mutual friend. We might greet each other as we passed in the hall or, if I were extremely lucky, be able to play hearts with her and two of her friends if we all had the same free period. I'll never forget when I shot the moon the first time I ever played, and in her own astonishment at my unintended coup, she let out an exasperated gasp/laugh with a big smile, her hair swinging ever so provocatively. Wow.

Despite being unsure if she had a boyfriend, I could never summon the courage to ask her out because I was a total loser. So my crush became an infatuation, and I felt great surges of adrenaline and other hormones every time I saw her. Lots of internal sighing ensued.

So there's the fanciful association. "That's All" always triggers a memory of Christine. You've just witnessed the unconscious part of the process. I needed an example for what I was going to write about for you, and while listening to some music, my unconscious mind triggered this memory.

But how do I make this into something universal, that everyone can relate to?

Making It Universal

Milch says, "In our recollection as artists, an uninterrupted sequence of associations is made available to us which, if carried out, may generate a premise for a story." The premise for a story is our reward for digging in our psychological dirt.

I must now follow the chain of associations triggered by this memory and not turn away when they become emotional or revealing.

So the song triggers a memory of Christine, which triggers other memories of her, and of me, and of high school. Somewhere in here are feelings to be explored. I must engage in a Socratic dialogue to delve within. This area becomes the conscious part of the process.

How did I feel in high school? Because I was in The Zone as I wrote the above recollection, I see that I felt like a loser, and still think of myself as such during that time of my life.

Why do I feel that way? I recall that I was not the snappiest dresser. I felt awkward around the girls. Okay, why? I was not confident. So what? Most high schoolers aren't. What else? I wanted something. I wanted to be close to her, to know her, to be with her. But despite that desire, I did not act. I did not have the courage to act.

Okay, I'm getting closer now. "I did not have the courage to act." Why? Because I was afraid, afraid of rejection, of the blow to my already fragile self-esteem. But *all teenagers are like this.* So what?

Darn it! Why didn't I have the courage? Why couldn't I have just asked her out?!

Ah. Now I've got it. Do you? Have I just found the universal common association?

I need to forgive myself. I need to forgive myself for who I was in high school. And who doesn't? We aren't fully formed human beings yet. Adolescence is widely regarded as a miserable time in life. And how much more universal can needing to forgive oneself be?

Most important, forgiveness has nothing whatsoever to do with Christine, the fanciful association. It goes to how I feel now about how I felt as a teenager. Forgiveness can certainly be the premise of a story. We all have a desire to go back in time to relive something, to fix something, to change how things turn out, to right the wrongs we ourselves were guilty of. It almost always is the result of regret, and regret can be healed only by forgiveness, usually of oneself.

So from the fanciful association of a Genesis song with Christine, I ended up at a premise about the need to forgive myself for how I felt about myself a long time ago.

So maybe the story is about a guy who goes back to high school to get the "one that got away"? Except that's not terribly original. In fact, it downright stinks as a story premise. How do I fix it? I must find another venue for a story, something with the same theme of forgiveness but set in another place or time or both.

Maybe you can help. Maybe you'll discover something about the African diamond wars that brings a new angle to this theme. Or it's a science fiction story. Who knows? It's up to your imagination. I sure haven't figured it out yet.

Taking the Pain Out of the Past

What else can we take away from this process you just witnessed? Milch quotes a teacher of his who says that, "This process that we artists undertake is the process by which everything which seems merely fanciful and is imprisoned in the past, in its seeming unrecoverability, is once again brought to life and conjugated into the future tense of joy."

In other words, we need to take these memories and associations that may be painful in some way, and by converting them into a universal story everyone can relate to, we create something bigger than ourselves, something that harbors resonance and meaning and, therefore, joy.

This creation is a combination of unconscious and conscious processes.

Look at Tim Kring's example. He took his experience of killing a deer and, through a series of imaginative associations, made it into a universal story for *Crossing Jordan*. He likely got there via The Zone, just as Vanessa did in Russell Banks's class. She said, "There are times when you're writing, and you don't remember what you've written, because you're just spaced out. And that whole story was that way. I did not know where it had come from." It came from a series of imaginative associations she was able to make universal.

Let's see how *The Shield* fits into this theory. I don't know Shawn Ryan well enough, but perhaps he'll forgive me if I speculate a bit. In unpublished portions of the interview, he made references to his limited physical stature as a child, and about how difficult it is to "feel like a whole man" when standing next to a member of the Delta Force. And who could blame him?

So Shawn may have taken a fanciful association of being a boy of small stature (pain of the past), and through a set of imaginative associations arrived at the iconic alpha-male character of Vic. He is a character who is deeply flawed, committed to personal and family gain, but torn by loyalty to his comrades and a sense of justice. These attributes are totally universal and relatable. Shawn then placed Vic into a venue that interested him intellectually, where these thematic interests could be explored.

I think Dan Bucatinsky, whom you will meet shortly, may be our best example of how the pain in its pastness can be converted to the future tense of joy. Dan initially believed the route to true creativity was to escape his present circumstances. As a youthful actor, he chose roles that would take him far away from himself. He later realized that his path lay in the opposite direction—toward that which he feared the most: the truth about himself. Dan accepted, and embraced, who he was. From that moment on, his true development as an artist began. His life transformed his work, and his work subsequently transformed his art.

All of these writers took the "me" out of their work and made it universal. You do so to find the truth in your work.

Why Truth?

So why is truth so important?

Ultimately, the creative process must be transformative for both artist and audiences; otherwise, it is merely an exercise in vanity or craft. Without transformation, the journey itself becomes pointless. Why end up where you started if you haven't grown in the process? Frodo Baggins returns to Hobbiton at the conclusion of *Return of the King* (Tolkien 1973, 476), but he has been greatly transformed by his journey.

But can you, the writer, seek truth in your material while still working in Hollywood? The collision between art and commerce often makes it difficult. Agents want their clients to specialize in something, so that they become the expert in a particular genre. Once this perception has been solidified, employment is more easily procured, for Hollywood employers seek comfort in the form of repeat successes driven by "experts." We'll discuss this idea more in future chapters, but suffice it to say that herein lies the challenge of television.

Further Reading

Lamott, Anne. 1995. *Bird by Bird: Some Instructions on Writing and Life*. New York: Anchor.

4

How to Be a Better Writer; or, Why That College Degree Matters

In the face of all the things you'll confront as a TV writer, how can you maintain creativity during the actual nonwriting work?

Look within.

You are the sum total of your experiences, so use them! Just because you call yourself a "writer" doesn't mean you must eschew your past.

There's no doubt that history's greatest writers were just writers. But many of them also lived extraordinary lives before they became authors. Others excelled in totally different occupations before discovering the written word.

In this chapter, we ask if using the skills, tools, or lessons from some other creative endeavor can augment one's writing. Do other creative outlets provide a natural synergy with writing? If so, which ones?

And another "why" question arises: why should I try some acting before, or when, I become a writer?

Suggested Viewings

Blind Faith: Frank Military
Heroes: "Pilot," by Tim Kring
Homicide: "Colors," by Tom Fontana

LARRY: I want to discuss creativity in general, and begin with those of you that are or were actors. You take a totally different approach to storytelling. Carol, what was your acting path?

56

CAROL BARBEE: I did theater in high school, I was a theater major at Wake Forest, and I have my MFA in acting from UCLA.

LARRY: What did acting fulfill for you?

CAROL: I think it had to do with that search for feeling, just as singing was. North Carolina is very conservative. Southerners in general are pretty polite, which often means they don't say what they mean. That's why there are so many southern writers, because we live in subtext.

LARRY: So it was this search for feelings, to feel, to fill that void that we all need, especially young people.

CAROL: And to learn human behavior.

LARRY: Where did your parents come down on this acting thing?

CAROL: My mother was very supportive. She said, "I don't understand what you're doing, but I'll help you." My dad was like, "What are you doing?" He was much older, and was raised on a farm where no one became an actor. But he came around and was very proud, but I think more so of my writing.

LARRY: Was writing something that you aspired to, or was it an accident?

CAROL: I don't know why, but I always thought I'd be a writer, although it did not occur to me to actually do it for a while. I had several producers from acting jobs say they wanted to read anything I ever did. I knew I was being offered a great opportunity, but at the time, I felt I did not have the life experience to write anything of substance. I really gained them through acting.

LARRY: You did some improv, Vanessa, did you not?

VANESSA TAYLOR: I did the Groundlings for two years. I went all the way through their program.

LARRY: What did you get out of them?

VANESSA: a) I am not that funny; b) I really, really love doing monologues and performing, but I don't care about sketch comedy or think it's funny. I also learned the brutality of comedy, which I never understood, and now could never work in comedy. The last course I took there, which is the course that's essentially the audition for their performing company, was one of the worst experiences of my entire life. It was the worst three-month period I may ever have been through. And that says much.

LARRY: Because?

VANESSA: Because it was the first time I had known complete and utter failure. And I knew it from day one. So it was like, okay, now you will fail. You will spend twenty-four hours a day for three months knowing you are going to fail, and failing.

LARRY: Did you feel you were being set up to fail?

VANESSA: I think I set myself up to fail because I was so frightened. But I just knew from the very beginning. I did a sketch the first day of class that I thought was an interesting concept, and it just got trashed. I thought, "Oh, my God. I'm just going to fail." I had gone very quickly through their program. I felt very positive. And suddenly it was all falling apart. I think I just crumbled.

LARRY: So did you take anything *positive* away from improvisation?

VANESSA: Improving monologues, which I've always loved. Now, as I go through scripts, I'm wandering through being each of the characters.

LARRY: Do you use your acting experience in a scene—finding objectives, that kind of thing?

VANESSA: I did take that from the Groundlings. Being economical. There is no dead weight in sketch.

LARRY: Dan, you and I grew up in the same town and went to the same high school. This is a fairly wealthy community just north of New York City. I find it interesting that, despite 90 percent of our graduating classes having gone to prestigious colleges and pursuing professional occupations, there've been a significant number of us that have found success in entertainment. It shows that you can't keep natural creativity repressed.

DAN BUCATINSKY: The creative process, by definition, is unsafe. Now, we creative people are constantly looking for safe places to play. But in a weird way, it's like there's a playground in the middle of Beirut. You create a little playpen for yourself if you have the need, regardless of where you live, I think.

LARRY: It isn't always safe to do, is it?

DAN: The creative process is unsafe because one minute you are enjoying playtime and finding out things and taking a journey, and the next you're either your own internal editor or self-doubt intrudes or the outside world is telling you you're bad and look fat in those jeans.

LARRY: So why acting?

DAN: Escape.

LARRY: From?

DAN: The process of coming out—I don't know how to describe it. It's very suffocating. Part of you wants to be suffocated so that you don't have to acknowledge the truth. I made a pact with myself that if I wound up being gay, I'd kill myself at eighteen.

LARRY: It'd be an understatement to say that that's an enormous amount of pressure to put on oneself.

DAN: Freshman year in college I thought, "Oh, shit. I'm nearing the deadline. I better not be gay." But in college I explored being creative for the first time, and that's what allowed me to write.

LARRY: Do you think that as an alternative to accepting the truth about yourself, to *expressing* that truth, that writing was a way to ease that transition?

DAN: Yes, and acting was, too. It was a great way to go to a different place, to be someone else. I was obsessed with being somebody else, anybody but myself. And I think that started really, really young. There was that awful feeling that I was not who everyone thought I was, or was supposed to be. So as a child, I played and created a make-believe world.

LARRY: So acting was important to you as an escape. Did writing ever cross your mind as a creative outlet before you really did it?

DAN: I fought it. The actor in me was frustrated by how little you are allowed to act, because you have to be hired to act. This led me to write as a way of creating acting opportunities for myself. Tenacity can lead to opening a new door for creative expression.

LARRY: I assume that you have found some fulfillment in writing.

DAN: Yes, it started out by making a movie, but that led to the TV thing. I would love to go back to making a movie. I've never felt more creatively satisfied in my life than I was when I was making my movie.

LARRY: Tell us why.

DAN: For a half-million dollars we spent twenty-eight days making the movie that I had written. The problems I had were the best problems in the world. It was purely what was on the page and what we had written. I was not serving a studio or a network.

LARRY: Is acting still an escape for you?

DAN: Creativity in general is addictive. You can't get enough of it. But what I get out of it now has to do with working a different side of my brain. Like working a muscle that has to do with accessing emotional places. It has to do with going to a place that I can't go to. I'm using a part of my brain and my soul that I don't use in my writing or producing or fielding calls, which is the bane of my existence. The actor gets to go inside the actual soul of a fictional character and make it come to life. And I contend that acting makes me a better writer, and writing makes me a better actor.

LARRY: Hart, you weren't an actor, but had another creative outlet.

HART HANSON: I dropped out of high school and joined a heavy metal band.

LARRY: Where did that come from?

HART: God knows, because I have *no* talent. Didn't find that out for years. I just had great enthusiasm for it. The funny thing is that I was seventeen years old, in this band touring western Canada, and we did not know it, but because of the advent of punk rock, we were already dead.

LARRY: So just one day you started playing music?

HART: Just played guitar one day in school and kept playing. Joined this band with all these people who were older than me. Then I hurt my hand—thank you, Jesus—so I put my guitar aside and went to university.

LARRY: That moment when you pick up that guitar, what are you reaching for?

HART: I just got lost in music. Like every dumb-ass kid my age, music was cool. I just had this overwhelming desire, like any other air-guitar player, to play it. But I actually had a guitar. I still play. I still suck. No talent. None.

LARRY: You were a big reader, too. Did making the music and reading fulfill something?

HART: Yes. I still feel it. I still have to know what the credit-sequence song is to any show I write. I need this feeling that takes me to a different plane. Music creates a 3-D space, like any good book or poetry, in a way that movies don't. It's more internal. I still use music when I'm writing something to get to a place where I want to make something, where I feel in my gut I can start to work. It's amazing how I can procrastinate until I find that.

Chapter 4 Lesson

You Can Take It with You

All television writers must embrace restrictions rather than recoil from them.

Aspiring writers, coming as they may from other vocations, might be intimidated because what they used to do was not in any way "creative." As a result, they may feel restricted or somehow limited in what they may be able to achieve. However, the bases of many other disciplines are often directly applicable to writing and, specifically, to television writing.

Here's an example. I know a writer who has a BA in chemistry. She worked in a pharmaceutical lab. After graduation, she went to film school, never intending to use her scientific background, or so she thought.

Once she became a regularly employed television writer, she discovered that one of her strengths was how to properly structure a story. For the vast majority of television programming, scenes must logically follow one another. The problem is that when you are in a Room with your fellow writers hashing the story out, you often come up with great ideas for scenes but have no idea where they belong in a story.

Some writers have a special gift for looking at a mélange of scenes and putting them in a dramatically interesting order. These scenes are often placed on index cards on a bulletin board. Some, such as this writer I know, may spend several minutes staring at all the cards and then suddenly shift them all around. It's not unlike a jigsaw puzzle. Only when the cards are in a certain order does the entire picture begin to take shape as a coherent storyline.

Where did this strange ability to structure scenes come from? It came from years of her studying math, physics, and chemistry. Her mind had been trained in these disciplines to think logically, to solve problems by moving one step at a time, and to determine the most concise method of solving any given problem. If one approach did not work, she would try something else, because there are often many ways to solve a complex math problem.

That's why that musty old college diploma hanging on your wall matters.

Objective: Acting

Actors really have an edge over people coming to writing from other disciplines. The actor who does his job right is the one who is so immersed in his process, he is not even aware there is an audience. He is so immersed in his character, in the scene he is portraying, that there is no other reality for him in that moment. He is living the reality of the scene.

He is living the *truth* of the scene. That's why acting experience can be such a powerful asset to you as a writer.

It was not surprising for me to learn that Carol Barbee ascribes to the Stanislavsky method of acting. In Michael Mills's explanation of the Method for the Actor's Studio, he describes it as requiring the performer to "draw on his or her own self, on experiences, memories, and emotions that could inform a characterization and shape how a character might speak or move. Characters were thus shown to have an interior life and not be a stereotype" (1998, 1).

Indeed, Carol improvises her way through the scene toward a specific goal, likely decided upon in an outline. Stanislavsky describes a character's goal in a scene as the "objective" (ibid., 121–39). It is the fundamental desire or wish the character is trying to achieve. Over the course of an entire story, these minor objectives serve the larger "superobjective," which, in the best of circumstances, contains the author's emotional purpose for writing the story in the first place. Whether that superobjective is achieved is dependent entirely on the action and conflict within the story.

The goal of improvisation, both from the actor's point of view and presumably Carol's, is to try different ways for each character to attempt to achieve an objective. By asking herself, "What would I, this character, do in this situation? Would I try this? Or that? Or X or Y or Z?" she is able to navigate the endless possibilities to find that which is most *true* to the characters. This process often leads to surprising discoveries or revelations in regards to both character and plot, and it's the main reason I prefer to work in this manner.

It is these surprising discoveries that help you find the truth to a character. It helps you understand *why* they want what they want.

If you've ever witnessed truly good improvisational sketch comedy, you've seen these moments happen before your eyes. Without any script to hang onto, an improvisational actor will spontaneously come up with some of the most outrageous ways to achieve her goal, while her partner will find equally ridiculous ways to prevent it. The key is not to think, but to act spontaneously. In other words, don't worry about being funny or thinking about what will be funny. That's focusing on product, which is the result.

Writers and actors should not care about results.

Instead, just do it. Let it happen. Just go with what comes into your head. Whether you are a writer or an actor, it's the process that leads the scene. So if your improv partner suggests something, such as the fact that an alien is sitting on your head, the cardinal rule of improvisation is to say, "Yes!" If you don't, the scene won't go anywhere.

Of course, you probably don't have a writing partner. So in that case, use the voice in your head. Let that voice say yes.

Using Acting Techniques While Writing

Almost all current American television utilizes the superobjective—a goal-oriented process—as its basis for storytelling. Yet few American television writers consciously use the method while writing.

The trick, of course, is that television writing is so restricted by enforced deadlines that you must quickly decide when enough angles have been tried to achieve an objective and a strong-enough scene exists to move on to the next one.

Thus, if a writer is able to meld any other activity that immerses him in human emotion—in feeling—all it can do is assist the work. It adds layers. It enhances dramatic interaction, saturating and shading the color of human drama in minute, yet impactful, ways. It tells you *why*. The more a writer dives into these other endeavors, the richer his work is likely to be. In some cases, your experience may simply become an asset to the craft of television. Oftentimes, writers will be hired because they specialize in one particular aspect of the entire process. Some people just have a good feel for a joke. Others come from a law enforcement background and can bring an air of authenticity to the creation of a story. Others are good with structure. Others are just bottomless wells of ideas.

You'll note that even though Vanessa thought she was terrible at improvisation, she took something useful away from that experience. Even though Hart thinks of himself as a terrible musician, his experiences still play a role in his work.

Get Out of the House

This point brings us to an uncomfortable topic. You can certainly become a great writer growing up under privileged circumstances, going to a top college, going to a legendary film school, and then getting an agent through some lucky connection. How much you will have to write about and how much depth that material has, however, may be where you meet your biggest creative challenges.

Generally speaking, people who have lived life under more challenging circumstances have more to write about, and do so with greater depth and understanding of the human experience. That's not to say that the more sheltered among us cannot achieve such greatness in writing. However, I urge any of you who have not ventured out beyond the confines of modern American life to do so. It will only strengthen your work, and your process, because you will be exposed to the truth of other people's lives.

Regardless, whether you came to writing through another art or through a chemical engineering program, don't just toss those experiences away. They will help you as you write.

Further Reading

Cameron, Julia. 2002. *The Artist's Way*. New York: Putnam.

5

How to Find Your Voice; or, Why Theme Is Important

The greatest compliment a writer can receive is that you have a particular voice. In short, it means that your work is somehow totally distinguishable as being yours, and yours alone. As we know, craft is something any writer can improve over time. Talent is innate, however. Some have talent and discover it in time to make something from it. Others may have talent but never discover it.

The question is whether voice, like talent, is a natural gift that requires discovery, or if it is something that develops as a writer matures. What exactly is a writer's "voice"? Where does it come from? How does it develop? Are there specific rules you follow to achieve what others describe as a "distinctive voice"?

I postulate a link between voice and theme. Writers often find themselves harping on the same topic. Maybe it's religion. Maybe it's violence. Maybe it's warm toast with butter. Regardless, the themes writers gravitate toward are the result of their soul's inner workings—their own spirit struggling with a particularly vexing issue. With each successive work, the examination of this theme takes on greater breadth and depth. Genres may change. The storytelling structure may alter. But the core theme remains the same.

Is it possible that by consistently working on a theme, which is deeply personal to a writer, a voice makes itself apparent in those moments when you are immersed in your work? Can voice emerge from theme? Finally, with respect to being on staff, can you find or maintain your voice when you are destined to have your work changed?

66

Suggested Viewings

Wonderfalls: "Pilot," by Bryan Fuller
Wonderfalls: "Pink Flamingos," by Aaron Harberts and Gretchen Berg
Deadwood: "A Two-Headed Beast," by David Milch

LARRY: Bryan, I detect similar themes in both *Dead Like Me* and *Wonderfalls*, themes that preoccupy myself as well.

BRYAN FULLER: Death and religion are things I like to explore. *Star Trek* involved intellectual ideas about the glory of exploration and how grand it was for the human spirit. That was nice, but not gripping on a personal level. That's when I wrote *Dead Like Me*.

LARRY: Where did the concept come from?

BRYAN: I remembered a Piers Anthony story, the title of which escapes me, that I read in sixth grade. I loved the idea of a mortal becoming Death. It's not an uncommon idea, but I thought, "Who would be the person that wouldn't want to be a grim reaper when they die?" The answer was that it was someone who was avoiding life to begin with, and has to do all the things that they were avoiding in life.

LARRY: Something reflective of yourself?

BRYAN: I think that's something universal. The question for that character is, "What are you going to be when you grow up?" and her answer is, "I don't know." Then she dies, and so it's forced on her as "You're going to be a grim reaper."

LARRY: Did any of that come from your experience growing up in that backwater town?

BRYAN: It came from my experience of being in L.A. after college, doing temp jobs, not knowing where my feet were going to land. And so all the temp jobs that George had in that show, I had as well.

LARRY: There're many similarities between George and Jaye and *Wonderfalls*. Was that intentional?

BRYAN: They were coming out of the same place in my life. They're similar in many ways. The big difference is that George is afraid that Jaye is lazy. George is avoiding life because she's afraid of responsibility. She doesn't want to grow up. She wants to be coddled, she wants to sleep in, and she doesn't want to have to be an adult. Whereas Jaye's going to do as little to get by because she just doesn't give a hoot.

LARRY: Why not? Is that something you were going to develop?

BRYAN: If you've met a contemporary teen or someone in their early twenties, most of them don't give a shit because they don't see what's to give a shit about. It's hard for them to see what to invest in when all the adults around them are miserable and unhappy. Why bust your ass to be unhappy when you can do very little and be unhappy? The art of laziness is how Jaye operates, and I think her punishment from the universe is, "You don't get to be lazy anymore, because we're going to drive you crazy." So that was her comeuppance for being a lazy person. George's comeuppance for fear was having the ultimate fear come true. Death bites her on the ass.

LARRY: Would that ultimately lead to redemption?

BRYAN: I think *redemption* is an interesting word. It feels too final, because it implies that the character's problems are in the past. I don't think we get rid of our problems quite so easily. I don't think redemption is as easy in real life as it is in storytelling.

LARRY: Did you have a targeted theme in terms of how George and Jaye were going to grow in each episode?

BRYAN: Both must grow in some way. I think George has a greater capacity for it, because eventually her fear is going to be whittled down. She'll have to do all the things someone her age has to do, she just is doing them as the undead. So those fears are going to apply to a first date, a first job, or being thrust into a situation that you don't know. You can overcome your fear in each situation, but there's going to be another one right around the corner that's going to be as anxiety inducing as the last one. So it's just a matter of becoming a fuller human being.

LARRY: And with Jaye?

BRYAN: Jaye's desperately trying to hold on to her laziness. I think her potential for growth is not as limited, but she's more resistant to growth than George is. But the great thing about Jaye is that she's got a hard heart. The first thing that's plopped in front of her is a romantic interest, when she thought it was not in the cards for her.

LARRY: I think you hit that magical target that reflects society, even though the show did not catch on, which I think had more to do with poor marketing than anything else. I spoke to a woman from my high school class who is now back at our school as a volleyball coach. I asked, "What changes do you notice between now and when we were in school?" She said, "When we were there, most kids had one or two after-school things that they were really devoted to and would excel at. Today they're doing seven or eight that they're all mediocre at in order to get into a good college." It leads to the question of how society's values seem to be so completely out of sync with what young people might be hoping to achieve.

BRYAN: I'm thinking they're also really desperate. Society's values are all over the map. It's probably always been this way, but it's hard for a kid to identify with one way of doing things and set on a path because there're so many different paths. If you're looking for a path and you see many of them, then you might not choose any of them. That was kind of the thing with George.

LARRY: What was the ultimate plan with Jaye?

BRYAN: That she is the new Jesus—a slacker girl with no clue. We were going to get there from a convoluted series of accidents where it appeared her sister had a miracle birth.

LARRY: Are the Muses real or only in her head, from your perspective?

BRYAN: I think because she has seen the concrete outcome of their influences she can say that they are real even though they may not be tangible, and even though they may only exist in her head.

LARRY: Would her attitude change if she accepted this?

BRYAN: I don't think she would ever entirely accept it. I think she was always going to be pissed off at them, like, making things inconvenient for her. It's like having a child. You can love your child and accept it, but if you want to go out on a Saturday night and can't find a babysitter, you're going to be a little resentful.

LARRY: I want to talk about voice, because I think it's linked to theme. I know when I read a Bryan Fuller script because you have a distinctive voice. You have this method of expression, which is reflected not only by your writing voice but in your personality. I want to ask Aaron and Gretchen, who worked for you on *Wonderfalls*, how they handled reconciling their voices with yours.

AARON HARBERTS: It's always difficult when you have someone with a unique voice like Bryan's, from the staff's point of view. It's impossible to replicate that voice. Nobody can do it.

GRETCHEN BERG: You want to try and do it, but Bryan always will have to take a pass.

AARON: He owns the keys to that car.

LARRY: Was it frustrating?

AARON: No, because we were all on the same page. Bryan never said, "This sucks, you idiot," because we all understood that he owned it from day one.

GRETCHEN: And he was appreciative, too.

AARON: He was so appreciative because it means much to a showrunner who both understands that his voice can't be replicated and that the work you do to get the story in place and the character's attitudes correct is valuable.

BRYAN: Very much so. It's all about expectations.

LARRY: Because we can't write in David Mamet's voice, we find other ways to make ourselves valuable. So, would you two classify your combined team effort as a singular voice?

GRETCHEN: I think so. There were times in our lives where we were considering separate projects, but we spent so much time developing the partnership's voice that it did get established. So I don't necessarily feel like I would enjoy writing by myself. I am curious to hear what my own voice is.

LARRY: Let's talk about developing voice. Does it begin with literature, Michael? Do you believe you have to be a voracious reader to be a great writer?

MICHAEL CHERNUCHIN: I personally don't believe there's ever been a great writer that was not a big reader.

LARRY: So were you influenced by other styles, subconsciously or consciously?

MICHAEL: I copied everybody. I wanted to be Fitzgerald. When I taught creative writing, I had the class do an exercise: "Everybody go home and read *A Farewell to Arms*" [1929]. Then I told them to write *Farewell to Arms* as if they were F. Scott Fitzgerald, and vice versa. Once you are able to copy another's voice, then maybe your own develops.

LARRY: Is that also a matter of gaining confidence in your own work?

MICHAEL: That, and just doing it. That's the greatest thing about being a TV writer. You can write a script and see it work, recognize that it did, and do it again—or vice versa.

LARRY: Do you think your voice contributed to television in some way, on the whole?

MICHAEL: One thing I think I added to the literature of TV was the reality of law. I don't think anybody had done that before I did it on *Law & Order*. There were legal shows, but they were not about the law. I think I made it understandable and did not cheat the audience, so the lawyers were talking like lawyers. That's something I observed by being a lawyer, and watching other lawyers.

LARRY: Jason, in your earlier work in plays, did you ever attack any common theme?

JASON KATIMS: My writing has always been about people's desires and attempts to connect in the world and to each other.

LARRY: Was it always there from the beginning?

JASON: I think so, yeah.

LARRY: Frank, as you write, do you feel that theme is going to develop on its own?

FRANK MILITARY: The best writing I've done happens when I allow it to come through naturally. The worst writing I've done is when I tried to force it. If the audience is watching your movie, they are going to absorb things, the same way the script is going to absorb them through your psyche when you're writing it. Just trust in it and get out of its way and not push it.

LARRY: This is similar to what Mamet says in his book *On Directing Film* [1991, 18]. He fights to string together shots that tell the story themselves. He doesn't try to make something "interesting." So, it's this organic approach that de-intellectualizes the process. Now, that's great for features, but in television, you don't necessarily have the luxury of time to let theme develop.

FRANK: That's not always true. Most showrunners, studios, and networks don't really care about theme unless it's intrinsic to the show's concept. So you may be able to take that approach. I know I have.

LARRY: Fair enough. I think it goes back to process. I find the theme first in the outline, and then refine it as I actually write. I find myself, like Bryan, coming back to similar things. Kim, are there themes that you keep returning to?

KIM NEWTON: I try to tell the stories that have impacted me. Being adopted, I've always wanted to do a good adoption story. Yet I find that the things that are closest to me are the things I can't do very well. A little detachment from a story is a good thing.

LARRY: Yes, one wrong move and you're into self-indulgence, of losing that universality Michael and Tim have spoken of.

KIM: I've also found that those really personal stories aren't the cathartic experiences I'd hoped. Some people are better about tapping into that. The other truth is that as a TV writer, you write so much and so often that you're bound to tell as many stories that you don't care about as ones you do.

LARRY: Neal, what themes do you enjoy writing about?

NEAL BAER: I like stories where people have a second chance, and they get them, because I love *Vertigo* [1958], which is about having a second chance. So we had a show where we asked, "What if a mother has lost her child, yet something inside her tells her the child's not dead, even though the child was killed in a car accident?" She gets a second chance, and she finds the child. It turns out that her eggs were stolen and that she has other children who look like this daughter who died. But she got a second chance. And that gets you.

LARRY: So why second chances? What about that hits you? Where is that coming from?

NEAL: I don't know. It just seems like it's this thing that we all want. And it's almost impossible to get.

LARRY: Jane, what are your common themes?

JANE ESPENSON: I don't come off as a dark, brooding person, nor am I in real life. Yet I write these very dark stories. I've always felt like I could go to these dark places, like serial killer stuff, without feeling touched by it. It always felt like Agatha Christie horror, where it was not real. I like the irony of it, this sunny little girl writing a dark short story. I liked the way it shocked the teachers.

LARRY: What about more emotional themes?

JANE: I gravitate to stand-alone episodes that take a minor character and put them at the center for an episode. I wrote a couple of episodes of *Buffy* that took Jonathan and Andrew, very minor characters, and made them the star of the episode. They are not supporting characters in their own lives, after all. They are the heroes of their own story.

LARRY: What about that gets to you?

JANE: I think so many people go through life thinking of themselves as supporting characters. And they're not, even that awkward kid in high school that you always thought of as tangential; in their own life they're stars.

LARRY: Is that coming from your own life?

JANE: I'm not prepared to say for sure, but I've certainly had these moments of revelation where a person who you'd always thought of as just a funny friend opens up to you and you realize, "Oh, there's a whole person in there." Definitely had that. I'm sure I've been that person, too.

LARRY: That's a very compassionate perspective to have.

JANE: Well, either that or it's awful. Nobody should have to learn that. We should all know that everybody's a person just the same as we are.

LARRY: Anything else along those lines?

JANE: I love to take a character and deliberately make them go out of character. I love writing the out-of-character lines to show that those minor characters have more aspects than we have given them. I'm tired of a small character having only one real strong character trait that you play in every scene. So Character X is the coward; he'll always have the cowardly line. I like to take that character and give him a brave line to show that everybody's brave sometimes. If there's anything that unifies my work, it might be that.

LARRY: Jason, do you think you were able to develop your voice because you had the opportunity to do so in a nonpaying environment?

JASON: During the years I was writing plays, it was really frustrating. I got a few smaller regional productions but never anything I could earn a living doing. But as difficult as those years were, I am very grateful that I had that time, when I could write whatever I wanted and nobody cared. I was not on anybody's radar, and that's a great gift, because once I came out here and started writing for a living, the pressure became enormous, and the goals were not pure, and there was not enough time. So I feel I had that time to develop a voice. That gave me a certain confidence. No, wait. I never have confidence as a writer—I always feel like an impostor—but that really served me well when suddenly I was in this very intimidating situation with brilliant writers and great actors.

Chapter 5 Lesson

Let's attempt to build a definition of voice from a few different building blocks. The first block we'll use is that *voice is a combination of syntax, vocabulary, diction, punctuation, and other functional elements of language to create a style unique to the writer.*

Next we focus on style. *Style is the substance that the form of the writing takes.* The style of what you are reading right now is intended to be scholarly because this is a scholarly text. The style of *Law & Order* is appropriate because it resides in the genre of cop and lawyer shows.

Finally, we return to imaginative associations, which we remind ourselves are emotional memories that you have made universal.

We combine these three elements to define voice as the *uncensored imaginative associations of the writer that, when expressed with a specific combination of linguistic tools, create a unique and identifiable source from which the work forms an emotional connection with the audience.*

How's that for a definition? But we needed to conduct that exercise in order to fully understand the importance of voice both to author and to audience.

Why is voice important? From an artistic standpoint, we want to constantly develop and transform our art. If we did not develop and transform our art, we would forever repeat the same material over and over. What's the point of being an artist if you do the same thing day after day? You may as well get a regular job. Plus, once you've found the truth in something, then you've understood its essence. There's nothing more to discover.

From a pragmatic standpoint, the development of a unique voice is what will make you stand out in Hollywood. As random as the business is, one thing is relatively constant: there is a dearth of writers with truly unique voices. I mean no disrespect to anyone. It's a simple fact, just as one is unlikely to find very many Salvador Dalís in any given large sample of everyday painters.

A voice is not *required* to secure employment because hiring decisions are made for random reasons. However, a unique voice does put one in the spotlight. And it is show business, after all, so you want that spotlight to help secure employment (which, of course, is not the reason you should be writing).

Developing Your Voice

How do you begin developing a unique voice, or even identify that you have one? When you begin writing, you have to start somewhere. It can be intimidating enough to feel that you have nothing to say, or don't know how to write, but to feel you must write in a unique manner is a real burden.

First, don't panic. Write in whatever style you choose. Michael Chernuchin has his students write in different styles as exercises. Every genre has its own demands for style. So just write. Experiment. It's similar to trying on different outfits at a clothing store. You did not design the clothes. You are just trying to see which style fits you best.

Michael Chernuchin returns to Shakespeare for inspiration. Indeed, writers look to many different sources for assistance. Our first attempts at writing often borrow heavily from those writers we admire. Michael did not shy away from that truth, and I think it's instructive that imitation is deeply ingrained in our genetics. It serves a definitive purpose in life and, by extension, art. Imitation is one of the building blocks by which we acquire language. Children will listen to, and try to communicate with, adults by imitating phonemes. What is art, *any* art, but a language expressed through its tools?

A sculptor learns how to use her hands to mold clay. A painter learns how to handle a brush. A writer learns how to string sentences together to express something. Gradually, the artist gains confidence. He learns advanced tools for his craft. And one day, he finds his voice.

The process of experimentation, utilizing the work of other successful artists as a foundation for your own, seems fundamental to the development of your own style. Outside of the occasional genius who is somehow connected to the extra-artistic plane—the Mozarts, David Lynches, and Shakespeares of our world—all creative people must begin somewhere before they can create something where nothing was before. As writers, we must learn the alphabet before putting together words!

There is no shame in it, but I think many writers are embarrassed or ashamed that their work borrows from others. I don't see anything wrong with it. Inspiration can often spring from someone else's idea or book or story, which is subsequently transmuted through the writer's personal experience and psychology. Indeed, if we are to believe that there are a finite number of story archetypes from which all stories emerge, then imitation and inspiration are unavoidable. What makes a work unique is the writer's personal voice, style, and ability to create an emotional connection with the reader (or viewer).

As you write more, your own style will start to emerge as you experiment with different linguistic tools. *You* will start to emerge. To carry on the analogy, you'll pair a bebe T-shirt with those pants from Nordstrom. Or that scarf from a thrift shop with an Oscar de la Renta dress.

You'll take things already out there, and emerge with something wonderful. Doing so is what an old acting teacher of mine refers to as "taking something, making it your own, and giving it away."

Eventually, somebody who reads your material may announce that you have a voice. That's the only way to know *externally* if you have one. Internally, you must simply act in faith. So although it would be great if people say you look great in that outfit you threw together, you are comfortable with your own self-image, and it shouldn't matter what they say. You have your own style. It's yours. Own it and be proud.

Theme

Theme is defined as *the unifying subject or idea of a story.* Theme begins with an intangible set of emotions that coalesces into a definable concept, which is subsequently pushed to the background, only to be brought forth by drama. As we've seen with our participants, some cannot even begin to write without knowing what that idea is. Others let it emerge.

One thing is certain: time is so limited and there are so many other structures imposed on the television process anyway that you become adapted to them, and thus your writing will by definition be impure. In addition, certain television shows will naturally lend themselves to certain themes, and therefore impose a structure. Cop shows often focus on the concept of justice. Loyalty is a subject of military dramas.

Sometimes a singular episode may have its own theme yet somehow remain consonant with the overall theme of a series. *Crossing Jordan*'s overarching series theme was about illuminating the life of someone who is dead. Dramatically, on the surface, it was also about finding justice for the victim. That's just the way the system works. You need to learn to work within it. The good news is that you will often be able to control what theme interests you because the bosses generally don't care, don't want to know, and don't have time to notice.

Voice and Theme Are Linked

Why is theme important? If a theme naturally emerges as you write, then it will be inextricably linked to your voice. Because you are connecting with the audience emotionally, the theme that develops should also resonate emotionally. The downside with intellectualizing that theme before writing is that you run the risk of making your work didactic. You want your audience to come away from the work *feeling* the theme, not *thinking* it.

To quote Abraham Kaplan's article "The Aesthetics of the Popular Arts," to have "a fully aesthetic experience, feeling is deepened, given new content and meaning" (1966).

Further Reading

King, Stephen. 2002. *On Writing*. New York: Pocket.

Mamet, David. 2000. *Three Uses of the Knife: On the Nature and Purpose of Drama*. New York: Vintage.

6

How to Embrace or Ignore Your Past; or, Why You Must Say Yes

So you are on the writing staff of a show. You are dealing with the realities of television. You have people talking about theme. Some of them seem to have amazing and original voices. They all write really great scripts. You may start to doubt yourself. You may wonder if you really have what it takes. You certainly wonder if you have any talent compared to your colleagues.

It's time to get to know your fellow writers. Start asking them where they came from, and if they had any special background that got them to this place. Why do you want to know this information? Because it will give you confidence. You will discover that you aren't so different from anyone else in Hollywood.

Writing is a tremendous challenge even for the most accomplished authors. Many people have an aspiration to write, but rarely set pen to paper because they are intimidated. They fear how their work will be judged. They worry that their command of the English language is weak. They don't believe they are creative enough. The list of internally generated reasons not to write is endless. You have probably experienced these reasons, and so has everyone else.

Should you fear that you may have no creative background or formal training? Do television writers all have a history of writing from an early age? Did any of the people I spoke to even have an interest in creative endeavors? If so, did it necessarily impact their decision to become a writer? If not, what drove them to write anyway?

Why did they become writers, of all things?

Suggested Viewings

My So-Called Life: "Life of Brian," by Jason Katims
NYPD Blue: "4B or Not 4B," by David Milch
Picket Fences: "Dem Bones," by Lawrence Meyers
Bones: "The Woman in Limbo," by Hart Hanson

LARRY: Let's see if an individual's background informed their choice to become a writer. I'm going to lay odds that it doesn't. First up is Carol Barbee. Did either parent do anything creative?

CAROL BARBEE: My mother was a singer in a gospel quartet at our local church. We did not have a kid's choir, so she put me in the adult choir.

LARRY: Church isn't where many kids want to hang out.

CAROL: Being from the rural South, childhood could be pretty boring. I did many art projects, by myself. But church—it had *feeling.* I could feel something through that music.

LARRY: Would you say that singing somehow brought you closer to God?

CAROL: Yes, it made me feel what it meant to be human, to be really connected to something.

LARRY: I think kids stretch to find something meaningful, to find their place in the world. I think they believe that computers and chat rooms somehow offer them that.

CAROL: Maybe they do, but I craved real interaction.

LARRY: Which you found, certainly in a spiritual way, in church. By the way, when I said that music brought you closer to God, I did not mean Jesus so much as the spiritual form God takes when you are doing something creative.

CAROL: Yes, exactly. I did not mean in a religious sense. I think those two things are totally separate. What it did was bring me closer to *reality,* that singing is human, that it's something alive. It's also why I eventually became an actor.

LARRY: Aaron, you also grew up in a church environment, but took something different away from it.

AARON HARBERTS: I'm an only child, and my father is a Presbyterian minister. My father was a writer because he delivered a sermon every week.

LARRY: Could his sermons have been an influence on you as a writer?

AARON: Yes, and beyond. I was privy to front-stage and backstage behavior. There's nothing zanier than a church. The characters that I met—the people I was exposed to because my mom was in the choir and my dad was at the pulpit—I was a six-year-old kid who was left to wander around. So I was exposed to all these different people that would come into my father's life. This is why I think I personally gravitate to comedy because there's so much comedy to be had just by observing human nature.

LARRY: Did you find any spiritual influence with your father being a minister?

AARON: Oddly, no. He's a very spiritual person and does much good, but I was also very aware that the dad who was at church was a minister—it was his job to help people, which is a different role from that of a father.

LARRY: Did your mother have a creative influence on you?

AARON: Very much so. She was a kindergarten teacher, and so she naturally was very creative. This was before video games, and we did not have cable TV or much money. So I just made do with what I had.

LARRY: Many of our colleagues had theater experience. Did you?

AARON: I loved plays. My mom pushed me into doing children's theater, and I really enjoyed that.

LARRY: Why?

AARON: Because I got to hang around other kids and thought it was so cool being onstage and doing these stories.

LARRY: Many actors talk about the synergy they feel with an audience and the attention they get as a child. Do you think there might have been some of that for you?

AARON: I really enjoyed becoming a different character, being part of a team. It was never about the acting.

LARRY: Gretchen, as Aaron's writing partner, it's notable that you had a totally different upbringing.

GRETCHEN BERG: My father is a chemical engineer but also a jack-of-all-trades. I think my parents are both skilled writers in their own way, but I don't think they would agree.

LARRY: What are your earliest memories of doing anything creative?

GRETCHEN: In second grade I wrote little books that I illustrated. One was called "The Mean Old Man," and these children banded together to beat the crap out of this man. My teacher was always asking me to stay after class, probably observing this disturbed kid who had all this repressed rage, to try and talk to me, and I'd say, "Leave me alone."

LARRY: Jason, you're from Brooklyn, which is a world apart from the Midwest. Did New York City affect you creatively growing up?

JASON KATIMS: My father was a salesman growing up, but he had been an actor. When he was fifty-five he started acting again. I did not even know he was an actor. I was playing in our unfinished basement one day, going through old boxes, and found old Broadway theater reviews of my father.

LARRY: How about your mother?

JASON: She was an English and philosophy major and did some teaching. Literature was a theme with my parents. We lived like normal people in Brooklyn, but there was much literature. My father would do Shakespearean soliloquies at the dinner table, and my mother loved poetry.

LARRY: Was there much storytelling in your household?

JASON: Much storytelling, irony, and humor. They're very political. They were very active in the civil rights movement, in the antiwar movement; they had lots of fund-raisings, demonstrations, and all that stuff was part of my moral foundation.

LARRY: Did you have creative instincts as a kid?

JASON: I was eight years old, and I wanted to make candles. I don't know where I got it from or why I wanted to do it, but my mother allowed it. I had this hot plate up in my room. She should not have let this eight-year-old kid melt wax with hot plates! I got all the equipment and molds, and I made these lousy lopsided candles that did not have the right coloring. But I always had this need to create things, and I did all sorts of weird stuff like that as a kid.

LARRY: We have another child of the sixties here, Tim Kring. Tim, you were right in the heart of those times.

TIM KRING: East Bay of San Francisco, in a very small little town called Pittsburgh, about 50 percent black. A very segregated environment, and it was a hotbed of the sixties.

LARRY: Were your parents active in that scene?

TIM: My parents were very progressive and supportive of the civil rights movement. My father was a mentor to lots of black kids on his high school track and field team.

LARRY: Did your folks have creative backgrounds?

TIM: No, it was not a particularly artistic household, but it was an intellectually stimulating one. My mother had a real strong tradition of Jewish intellectualism.

LARRY: So was there anything that pushed you in an artistic direction?

TIM: The family dynamic is an important component. I have two brothers. The elder was a real achiever, and the other was very creative, an independent thinker, with an artistic personality. I think I was really influenced by him. He was very influential in the way he looked at the world.

LARRY: Given the historical context, do you think you became more individuated at a younger age than most?

TIM: It's an interesting soup, and it has to do with times and being in San Francisco. But I was a spacey kid, sensitive and dreamy, and was left to be in my own head, and be an observer. I was trying to carve out some space in the family that was my own. A big part of it is that I was clearly learning disabled, some form of dyslexia, which pushed me farther into a dreamy internal life. My successes weren't found in academia. I could not compete there, and so EQ became more important than IQ—figuring out how to get what I want by being verbal as opposed to testing.

LARRY: Sticking with this intellectual background, I want to turn to Michael Chernuchin. Was there always a desire to write, to express?

MICHAEL CHERNUCHIN: Since I was eight. My parents took me to Arthur Miller's *All My Sons*. Most people go to a play, see the actors, and say, "That's what I want to do." I had no desire to be onstage; I wanted to be the one who wrote it.

LARRY: Where did the urge to express come from?

MICHAEL: I'm not really sure. The closest I can come to understanding it is something William Faulkner said in his Nobel Prize speech. He said, and I'm paraphrasing, "I wanted to create something where nothing was before." It's just something I always wanted to do.

LARRY: Could it come from the natural instinct of a child to create something, make it personal, and imprint it on the world?

MICHAEL: I never thought about that. I just wondered why my friends in New York with these amazing careers don't have that same need I do.

LARRY: Vanessa Taylor is a good friend of Carol Barbee's. They also share an acting background. Vanessa, did you do any writing as a youth?

VANESSA TAYLOR: When I was younger, I wrote fairy tales. But as I moved into actual short-story writing, it was more psychological, less escapist. I think it was a very profound loneliness that needed expression. At that age, whom are you going tell about that sort of thing? So writing kept me company in a way.

LARRY: Was there any other artistic expression?

VANESSA: From age twelve, I pursued acting and singing, which I did for more than ten years.

LARRY: What were you seeking?

VANESSA: At first, what many people are seeking, which is attention, affection, and affirmation. Having had a very lonely childhood, I was looking to be loved writ large. By the time I got to L.A., I was twenty-five and realized that I cared more about success than I did about acting. I did not believe I was ever going to be successful at it, so I let it go. By then, I did not need the same things from it anymore.

LARRY: Did you develop a respect for the process by seeing your mom so devoted to her profession?

VANESSA: I certainly developed a respect for discipline. I also went to the Interlochen Center for the Arts in Michigan, and it was about how to pursue the arts in a disciplined way.

LARRY: Neal Baer is a practicing physician. Neal, what else is in your background?

NEAL BAER: My father's a surgeon, and my mother was very active politically. I just always loved stories.

LARRY: Was storytelling a big part of your household growing up?

NEAL: I read much when I was a kid. I'm the oldest of six, and so I was the teacher.

LARRY: Were you encouraged creatively?

NEAL: I loved my French teacher. She was very cool—taught us all the Beatles' songs and Petula Clark songs in French. I also loved mythology, won the Mythology Bowl in seventh and eighth grades.

LARRY: Let's cut over to the rolling fields of the Midwest now. Jane Espenson hails from there.

JANE ESPENSON: I was born and raised in Ames, Iowa, which is this little college town, a wonderful place to grow up, very safe; we never locked the car or house. On autumn days you could hear the university marching band practicing across town. Idyllic, but it's the Midwest, so it's full of mosquitoes, and it's too hot or it's too cold.

LARRY: I sense an escape to television in here.

JANE: Definitely. I stayed in and watched all the great shows from the seventies. I knew which shows were good and which were bad. I remember saying to my mom that I loved *Barney Miller* [ABC, 1975–82] because I knew what those characters would do in any given situation.

LARRY: How old were you when you said that?

JANE: Eleven.

LARRY: Okay, a born writer.

JANE: I knew I wanted to write for TV. The way I fell asleep at night was to pick a show and imagine a little story and what all the characters would say. So I would write TV in my head to put myself to sleep at night.

LARRY: Anything creative from the parental side that might have encouraged this?

JANE: My mother had studied literature in college. Both parents read much. We're the sort of family that sits in silence for hours if we all have a book in our lap.

LARRY: Did your mom actually encourage television writing?

JANE: She encouraged me to write stories and poetry, but television—I don't think she really thought of television shows as things that were products of writers. She thought of them as products of Hollywood.

LARRY: And your father was a professor.

JANE: He was very much into the raw materials of academics, and my mother was into the measurements of academics.

LARRY: Raw materials like problem solving, which maybe played a part later in your life in breaking story for television.

JANE: Very much so.

LARRY: Let's stick with the influence of television growing up. I know it was important to me, primarily as a source for escape. How about you?

JANE: I don't think it was an escape; it was simply, what else was I gonna do? After school, I'd be sitting down between three thirty and five when my parents got home and watch TV, do homework, and back to TV by seven when prime time started in central time. I was an only child; there were very few distractions in our quiet, orderly house. My parents would read silently. I could sit, pick up my book, or do my homework. So I would sit quietly in the room with them, which was perfectly lovely, or I could go watch television.

LARRY: Is anyone going to back me up on the concept of TV as an escape?

BRYAN FULLER: I will.

LARRY: Excellent. What part of the country did you grow up in?

BRYAN: Eastern Washington State. My hometown has the distinction of having the highest percentage of welfare recipients per capita in the state.

LARRY: What were your feelings towards that area?

BRYAN: I could not wait to get out. It was bleak and dull. I understand now that there's a drug problem, and it's probably related to the fact that there isn't much else for kids to do besides go bowling, rent a movie, do drugs, or drink. I was not interested in either of the two latter things, so I just watched TV all the time.

LARRY: As an escape?

BRYAN: Totally. I worked at the movie theater and video stores. I bought a beta VCR in seventh grade.

LARRY: Looking back now that you're a writer, do you think that the amount of television and movies that you watched gave you a sense of storytelling?

BRYAN: Absolutely. That's what's so great about having seen so much television and movies. You pick up how people talk. You get used to the way stories are told.

LARRY: Was there any artistic bent in your family?

BRYAN: No. I can answer that quite definitively.

LARRY: Was writing a part of your life growing up?

BRYAN: Not at all.

LARRY: And were science fiction and fantasy early interests more than any other genre?

BRYAN: Absolutely. Horror first and foremost. *Star Wars* [1977] was very impactful, of course. *Alien* [1979] was the perfect hybrid of science fiction and horror, and that's actually the movie that had probably as big an impact as any.

LARRY: Let's stay out in the sticks for a bit. Shawn Ryan grew up in Illinois. Was it as idyllic in the Midwest as Jane described?

SHAWN RYAN: I grew up in Rockford, Illinois, a medium-sized city, about ninety minutes from Chicago. And yes, I had a very idyllic childhood. Although nobody here is copping to it yet, I hear all kinds of writers who had this awful childhood, the overbearing mother, the cavaliering father, and everything they write springs from that. In my case I had a very good family upbringing. I was always playing sports, always had something to do. I was a very happy child.

LARRY: What did your parents do?

SHAWN: My mother's a schoolteacher. My father is a CPA.

LARRY: Were you influenced by television?

SHAWN: I was one of those kids addicted to television, a big fan of the 1970 sitcoms.

LARRY: How about the theater? Would you go to Chicago?

SHAWN: Musicals were big. I saw *Annie* in Chicago. But Rockford had something called the New American Theater Company, which would do the high-profile dramatic plays after they'd been on Broadway. I became interested in theater, although my main passion was soccer, along with hockey and basketball.

LARRY: So it doesn't sound like you used TV or theater as an escape. But I'm wondering if there was, for lack of a better term, a quirk in your upbringing that—

SHAWN: Yes, something at an early age that gives you this instinct for imagination in writing. For me, although I was a very good athlete, I was very small for my age. I was the shortest kid through my sophomore year, girls included! I was not strong. I was not big. I was easily physically intimidated. Even though I was a regular athlete, I looked two years younger than my actual age.

LARRY: So that created some kind of creative imprint.

SHAWN: It must have, emotionally. I had this weird double existence where I was the little guy in the big world, but then I'd go off and play a soccer game and I would be the jock. It was kind of odd, so maybe that was where my writer tendencies came from.

LARRY: I was small, too, and I found that because I could not deflect confrontation physically, I'd rely on skilled diplomacy. It usually failed, of course, but still . . .

SHAWN: We're the same. I sought ways to avoid confrontations, and the easiest way to do that was to understand other people's perspectives. And that's intrinsic to my writing. If I have a scene with several characters and they all have different points of view, it's easy for me to see all sides.

LARRY: Did all your television viewing help you understand stories?

SHAWN: It helped create a gauge for what was good and what was not. I think the best thing one has as a writer is a bullshit detector that tells you when your material is not quite there, which is most of the time.

LARRY: Let's see how life treated youngsters in other countries. Javier Grillo-Marxuach is a product of Puerto Rico.

JAVIER GRILLO-MARXUACH: I was born in San Juan and lived in Puerto Rico until I was ten.

LARRY: And what were your parents doing in Puerto Rico?

JAVIER: My mother was a full-time mother, and my father was an oncologist.

LARRY: Was there storytelling?

JAVIER: They took me to many subtitled American movies. I also always had my nose buried in a book. I was a kid, who during recess went to the school library.

LARRY: Why?

JAVIER: Puerto Rico is a very hot country, and the school library was air-conditioned. I did not like sports or the mentality of athletic kids, so, really, the library was pretty much my only refuge.

LARRY: So you read much, but from where did creativity spring?

JAVIER: Well, Larry, I was a pale, fat kid, growing up in a very hot country. So I'd just play with my Legos or draw all day . . . but it was not just about that—I always had this restlessness to create something. It's an impulse, and I don't know where it came from. It's something I've had my whole life. I don't like being idle.

LARRY: This idea of not being idle—do you think that is because your dad was always working?

JAVIER: My father is one of the hardest-working people I know. He is genuinely committed to helping out cancer victims, and it's not just something he does for a living; it's something that he does for a *passion*. My father's goal in life, he'd always said, was to cure cancer.

LARRY: When you came to America, did things change for you creatively?

JAVIER: Yes. I have no way of knowing how I might have turned out had my family stayed in Puerto Rico—I would have probably found myself just the same there as I did here—but at the time, and at the young age of ten, I truly bought into the myth of the United States as "the land of opportunity."

LARRY: Did you hold America in high regard?

JAVIER: America was held up very highly, probably to an unrealistic level. I wanted to experience American movies, TV shows, and music. I really wanted to learn English, reading, and writing—those were important to me. I had the *World Book Encyclopedia* and had read the entire thing by age ten: that it was in English and an object from this far-off and mythical place was incredibly influential. I think I needed that escape. It's no slam on Puerto Rico, but I just did not really fit in that well as a kid. That encyclopedia, and *Star Wars*, represented another world I could escape to. I think that that need for escape was really serviced by those blockbusters of the late seventies.

LARRY: Swinging north to Canada, we have Hart Hanson.

HART HANSON: I grew up in Vancouver Island, as did my mom. Mining, logging, blue-collar background. Dad was a salesman, mom a secretary. Dad sold pharmaceuticals. My natural siblings were all within seven years of each other, being a Catholic family.

LARRY: So the family was religious?

HART: Yes, very. That's where Catholics get their building blocks about how the universe works.

LARRY: Carol Barbee found a spiritual connection in church through music. Aaron Harberts found characters. Did biblical stories stick with you on a narrative or spiritual basis?

HART: For certain. The Catholics know what they're doing. The catechism is so full of metaphor. You hear stories, go through it to figure out what it means, and learn what God wants you to get from that story.

LARRY: Your family moved much. My first thought is that a child would want to anchor himself, maybe with stories.

HART: All the moving made me a reader. The library was a real haven, and I was the only reader in my family.

LARRY: Do you gravitate towards any genre?

HART: The first thing I read were the myths. I read slices of history.

LARRY: So we have another avid reader. That seems to be another theme. Let's get grounded now and turn to Bob Singer. Bob, you really had a taste for city life early on.

ROBERT SINGER: I grew up in Nyack, New York. I was a journalism major at NYU, and got a job on a newspaper during the summer of my junior year. I left school early, but when I found that I was not gonna write like Jimmy Breslin, it was very depressing.

LARRY: So there was a bona fide interest in journalism?

ROBERT: I loved Breslin, Pete Hamill, and Red Smith. I wanted to do that. I read a Breslin column, this fantastic story about the Irish and police and drinking, and I thought, "Wow, you know, I don't think I could do that."

LARRY: Was it the detail that so intimidated you? Was it the fact that he had a voice?

ROBERT: Well, his voice was great. But the intimidating thing was that he took an incident and made it into a sociological study of the condition of Irish and police. I was blown away about this idea of a newspaper guy being able to turn this sort of cut-and-dry incident into something much bigger than that. I did not know if my mind actually could work that way.

LARRY: Did you pick up anything while you were at the paper?

ROBERT: I think it shows in my scriptwriting, in that I tend to be pretty succinct. Not flowery in the stage direction. I like to infuse it, when appropriate, with some humor. And the dialogue is fairly sparse. But I've always been more interested in what characters don't say than what they do say.

LARRY: What about being in the greatest cultural mecca in the world?

ROBERT: I was hardly an intellectual about it. Symphonies and operas weren't part of my upbringing. I mean, it was the *sixties*! New York was just spectacular. Frankly, it was post-Pill and pre-AIDS. You could not do better than that! I'd play rock and roll, and the music scene in New York in those days was unbelievable.

LARRY: So you're a musician.

ROBERT: Oh, I used to sing with doo-wop groups when I was in high school. And then I went to college and learned to play bad guitar and blues harp and sing. But I'd just play in bands in toilets in New Jersey or fraternity parties.

LARRY: Had there been any history of your family having any creative instincts?

ROBERT: Not a bit. My father owned a men's clothing store. My mother was a housewife.

LARRY: So there you have it: Bob Singer, rakish youth!

Chapter 6 Lesson

"Yes"

In examining the interviews, all writers should take heart. The writers interviewed here feel like a traveling group of artisans. There were singers, actors, wax melters, readers, poets, mythologists, artists, and newspaper readers. Some wanted to escape their dreary surroundings and developed interior worlds. Some just had an uncontrollable desire to create something. Their parents were teachers, gospel singers, artists, ministers, engineers, actors, activists, intellectuals, doctors, surgeons, and stay-at-homers.

This anecdotal evidence suggests that being a writer has nothing to do with where you are born, whether you write as a child, what your interests are, what your parents did, whether you eat peanut butter as a kid, or whether you have any encouragement.

There is, however, one thing they all do have in common. When opportunity knocked, they accepted the challenge. They said yes.

"Yes." It is the single most important word for any writer.

What every writer, and every artist, will find throughout their lives is that there are powerful forces that will discourage them from pursuing an artistic endeavor. Those opponents may include your own egos or internal doubting voices. You may have every advantage—an interest in writing, a mentor, loads of experience to draw upon, a flair for describing life's little moments—but if you let pass the moment when pen must be set to paper, then none of it matters.

So this idea of pedigree, or lack thereof, is an illusion. It's an obstacle. It's just another excuse offered to any aspiring writer to say no. I'll discuss the psychological underpinnings for why people get caught in this trap in the next chapter.

The other impediment that aspirants face is that some think they aren't emotional people. They don't wear their hearts on their sleeves, so how could they put them on the page? Some people think they are born comedy writers, good with a joke but not with real human interaction.

What of the writer who is highly attuned to the emotional plane of human existence? Will she fail at a procedural drama or a sitcom? For that matter, can a meat-and-potatoes craftsman write an emotionally compelling episode of a highly charged melodrama?

The degree of emotionality within each writer runs the gamut. Some writers, regardless of gender, are moved by the slightest heartfelt moment in a scene. Others remain as hard-hearted as the Grinch, and can write shows that have no place for emotion. The difficulty, but also the blessing, of working in television is that different shows require different styles of writing. *CSI* focuses more on plot and cool scientific methods, *24* relies almost exclusively on plot-driven suspense, and *Deadwood* (HBO) was elevated to different heights because of its starkly drawn characters and use of language. Meanwhile, sitcoms are mostly about the jokes.

Every writer has strengths and weaknesses. One of the most important things you can learn is how far your competence extends. It is one of the hardest lessons to learn because it forces you to admit failure. Yet the ability to admit failure not only builds character but also allows us to spend time on what we can achieve as opposed to things that are out of our reach. As humbling as such an admission may be, writing is as much about recognizing limitations as any other pursuit.

Ultimately, what matters is saying yes—to effort, to finding your strengths, and to accepting your weaknesses.

Getting to "Yes"

Why do you wish to write, particularly for a compromise-laden medium like television? *Why* do you want to get to "yes"?

So far the answers have to do with finding truth, finding meaning, and taking transformative journeys as both artists and people. You'll note that "making money," "fame," and "winning awards" are not on this list. That's because those reasons are superficial and will not serve you well at all. In such a difficult medium as television, those reasons will not sustain you in the hardest of times.

There is yet another deeper "why" to explore. This one is about understanding that the quest for truth, meaning, and transformation must be driven by purity of motive. Otherwise, your work will feel false and will be just plain bad.

Let's view these issues through the prism of child psychology and, in particular, the concept of expression from the childhood years. Again, it isn't something that our writers are conscious of but is buried within their respective psyches.

As children, we really aren't able to process emotions. They just happen to us. The nine-year-old child is all about egocentrism. Expression is about making an imprint on the world, about seeking attention, and about asking for love. The motive to create is not pure. Children *want* something extrinsic to the creative process itself. They want love or approval.

If you desire to become a writer for the accolades, for income, to please a parent, to feel important, or for any reason that begins with the phrase "I want," then you are no different from the child. You seek something exclusive of the writing process that the writing process absolutely will not fulfill. It won't. I guarantee it. You are chasing things that lie outside the realm of art. You are asking for disappointment. You must say no for the time being and reassess.

Now, let's look at how things change when you become an adolescent. From that period to the early twenties, you experience raw emotions for the first time while also having some processing capability. Take a moment and recall the first times you felt those emotions—the first infatuation, the rush from a first kiss, the anger at an authority figure, the first home run, even the first ride on a roller coaster.

At that age, we have not yet become cynical about feelings, nor have we developed defense mechanisms. We are sponges, soaking up every moment of new emotion, and, by God, some of those feelings are the most powerful things we have ever felt in our short lives. No longer children, we can express how we feel, but those expressions are irrational and explosive. Still, those feelings give us a rush. Exhilarating, but too powerful for us to handle.

Many people in this age group need to express what they feel. They just have to. They must get it out. To their friends, in chat rooms, on Facebook, in text messages—they just need to get it out, and get it out now.

This need is near purity of motive. This need is near purity of process. They aren't looking to win the senior-class award for writing. They don't want accolades. They just need to get it out. That's a pure desire to express.

If you want to become a writer for that same simple desire to express, and to revel in the *act of expression*, then you are ready to say yes. You must be a bit careful here, because the young person's motives for expression include a desire to be heard. That motive isn't pure, but it doesn't necessarily contaminate the process, either.

Why It Can't Be about You

What we will learn later is that television is about process, not product. Whatever grand vision you have for your particular episode of a show will very likely not make it to the screen. A version of it will—some more derivative of the original than others. However, the truth about television is that many things change from a story's initial conception to its final form. You must love the process and all it entails, because that is the part that you have some control over, and it will also prove to be the most fulfilling. You will have varying levels of control over the final product, but almost all control will be in the hands of other people (not all of them artists).

Recall what Michael Chernuchin said when I asked him where the urge to express came from. He paraphrased William Faulkner's Nobel Prize acceptance speech. Faulkner's actual words speak to the necessity to focus on the work—in other words, the process: "I feel that this award was not made to me as a man, but to my work—a life's work in the agony and sweat of the human spirit, not for glory and least of all for profit, but to create out of the materials of the human spirit something which did not exist before."

Further Reading

Keyes, Ralph. 2003. *The Courage to Write: How Writers Transcend Fear.* New York: Holt Paperbacks.

7

How to Start Writing;
or, Why Writer's Block Is Bunk

Now that you've learned that your fellow writers really did not come from some Writers' Utopia, hopefully you are feeling better about your own qualifications. However, all writers are plagued by doubt. This point is especially true when you are on your first show. You may start to wonder if what you are writing about has any value. Maybe you recall your first efforts at writing—clumsy, poorly structured, lacking focus, and maybe even a bit immature.

Maybe these doubts plague you so badly you develop Writer's Block. Uh-oh. What to do?

First, turn to your colleagues. In my case, I asked our panel about their first project and how they generated their first ideas, to see if they were moved by a need to express something from personal experience, or something else.

In addition, many writers, both new and established, have their hopes and dreams dashed when they actually get up the nerve to write something and it's terrible. The truth is that very few of us are born Hemingways; just as few musicians are born Mozarts. Life is about learning, and it takes decades just to master any craft.

So I also asked everyone about how successful they think their first works were, and what each took away from the experience.

Hopefully, this will help you understand that you aren't different from anyone else. I'll also tell you how to defeat Writer's Block, which can be understood only when you know why it exists.

96

Suggested Viewings

Picket Fences: "Heart of Saturday Night," by Ellen Herman
Twin Peaks: "Lonely Souls," by Mark Frost
Deadwood: "Here Was a Man," by Elizabeth Sarnoff

CAROL BARBEE: My first screenplay was called *Madonnas of the Field*.

LARRY: What was it about?

CAROL: Two female photographers during the Depression. The younger one is traveling with her mentor, and it was about what it was like to be close to one's hero. But it was also about motherhood and art.

LARRY: So was this a combination of research and life?

CAROL: Yes. I was always struck by the question of, "How was it that women held these positions, especially during the Depression?" I also became a mother while I was writing it, so it became a very real subject for me.

LARRY: So finding things that moved you emotionally were the keys to the piece. As a former actor, were you also able to draw on that experience for your first writing attempt?

CAROL: What's great about doing acting and then becoming a writer is in the theater you build a character incrementally. Every nuance, every movement—you try them all out to see what fits best, and in the process you create someone from the ground up and know them pretty well.

LARRY: So before tackling that first script, you drew on something that was directly applicable to writing. This is very similar to Dan Bucatinsky. Dan, tell us about your angle.

DAN BUCATINSKY: I wrote and starred in a one-act play. Two characters, sketchlike. It was really about turning expectations on their heads. It was about a guy who wanted to settle down and get married and a woman who was battling an alcohol addiction, who was playing the field and did not want to settle down. I liked the idea of seeing the genders in untraditional roles.

LARRY: How was that first work fulfilling?

DAN: It was about exploring who we are with relationships and how fear keeps us from moving forward. But it was not until I adapted that play into a movie about a gay couple that it was truly cathartic. Then I was really writing about something truthful. I was already with my partner for many years, but when I came out to L.A. I was very closeted.

LARRY: So like Carol, something came from within.

DAN: It happens when you are really not afraid to put it all out there.

LARRY: Persistence is critical for anyone in the arts. Sometimes it helps if you find what you want to do, and you just go for it. That sounds like your story, Jane.

JANE ESPENSON: I wrote a spec episode of *M*A*S*H* when I was twelve.

LARRY: All that television you watched planted a seed. What was this first spec about and why that of all things?

JANE: There was an interview that appeared in the *Des Moines Register* about writing for the show and how they sometimes buy specs. I'd always loved entering contests, so I figured, why not?

LARRY: Keep going with that—there's something there.

JANE: I loved to be singled out whenever I did something really well, to get a reward or praise. My mother was very interested in the idea that I wanted to be the first person to do any particular thing.

LARRY: Determination grew out of a desire to be singled out. So something external can drive one to pursue something they have an interest in?

JANE: And, in fact, I did win a contest with the *M*A*S*H* script.

LARRY: What was it about?

JANE: A woman wartime photographer shows up, and Charles realizes she is the woman who he's expected to marry, this upper-class thing. She had become a reporter and followed him out there. But now that she had tasted this independent life, she doesn't want to marry him anymore.

LARRY: I'd say that's pretty mature for twelve.

JANE: *One Day at a Time* was a big influence, stories of young women discovering their at-home life was not for them.

LARRY: Hart, you tackled prose before screenplays. Tell us about those first efforts.

HART HANSON: I had read much of Reynolds Price, Truman Capote, and Carson McCullers, so I just copied them.

LARRY: Aren't all our first stabs just emulating someone we admire?

HART: I hope so. I sure did. Part of it was hearing the thoughts about my work from people I respected—this was my first writing class. Even if it was not about me, I just wanted to participate. It was just so new.

LARRY: Any themes in those early stories?

HART: I constantly wrote about community and family pulling together.

LARRY: Did that come from moving thirteen times?

HART: Yeah, having to re-create our world each time.

LARRY: Tell me about your first big project.

HART: I had written a novel for a university class and won a national award, but it did not get published.

LARRY: Was it personal in any way?

HART: No, that was the problem with it.

LARRY: Did you feel that writing gave you an outlet for expression? Was that what you were searching for?

HART: I felt it was a way of explaining things to myself. I wrote one short story when my son was three, and I drove down to someone's house. We were together for hours in the car, and he kept noticing things. He'd say, "Is that a tornado?" I would answer, "No, it's a dust demon," and he asked, "Will it knock over the car?" So not until I wrote the short story about a guy who was not me, and a son who was not my son, in a relationship that was not ours, was I able to explain what this trip meant to me.

LARRY: Vanessa, you also discovered prose writing. After graduating Princeton, what happened?

VANESSA TAYLOR: I went for a year to Switzerland because I had a Rotary scholarship, and I focused on my writing. I ended up writing a short story about my experience in Switzerland that took six years to write.

LARRY: What was it about?

VANESSA: In Switzerland, my neighbor was twenty-eight, from Argentina. He'd come to Switzerland seeking a better life, and became a paperboy to support his studies of classical guitar. So he became my boyfriend, and I was fascinated by the life of an immigrant in Switzerland. He spoke decent French, but not great, but no English. I spoke decent French, but not Spanish. There were so many levels of not communicating in this relationship.

LARRY: What was the theme?

VANESSA: Trying to be the savior of another person, but not being able to even cross the divide that separates them, let alone fix their problem.

LARRY: Who influenced you as a writer?

VANESSA: I fell for this monologist, Josh Kornbluth. He was my muse. And at Princeton, I ended up in Russell Banks's class. I wrote a story set in the Deep South. It had a strange tone that was different from me. It was essentially about the misery of an impossible choice.

LARRY: Jason, was prose your first writing attempt?

JASON KATIMS: I wanted to be a songwriter, which was my first love. I stumbled into writing in college when I took a composition class. The teacher had us keep a journal. I read this journal entry one day, and she said, "That's a short story." It got me going on the idea of writing.

LARRY: So the journal writing was obviously personal. Was there a need for personal expression?

JASON: Writing has always been a way of communicating, and it's been a way of finding a voice. I'm one of those people who will always write. It's so a part of my life that if I have a few weeks off, after a while I have to sit down a few hours a day to focus on something.

LARRY: It's part of your DNA at this point.

JASON: It really is a part of my life. It's a weird thing, because it is what I do for a living, but it's also part of what makes me me.

LARRY: Tim, was writing your first form of expression?

TIM KRING: No, visual. I was the school photographer and was really affected by photography and cinematography. My love of film was born out of wanting to create beautiful images. Cinematographers fascinated me, and those were certain heroes of mine. I'd go to a movie based on their work more than anything else, and that was the impetus for taking a film class in junior college.

LARRY: That cannot be overlooked. Writers may not find themselves writing initially. They may stumble into it. Shawn, what kind of stuff did you do?

SHAWN RYAN: I had no interest in writing, but I had this interest in theater and took a course freshman year. The final project was to write a five-minute scene and grab other people from the class to act in it.

And I wrote this thing that was a juvenile rip-off of existential stuff. The professor came up to me afterward and said, "I'm teaching a play-writing class next year, and you really should sign up for it."

LARRY: And did you?

SHAWN: Soccer practice started at 4:00, and it would've made me late twice a week. But the coach said to take the class. I think my place on the soccer team suffered, but it exposed me to playwriting. The professor chose my play to produce, and I saw this play I had written performed. I was bitten by the bug.

LARRY: Gardner, was your first material dramatic or pragmatic?

GARDNER STERN: I did some creative writing in high school, and I started writing ads for an indie agency. I really enjoyed that and became a copywriter.

LARRY: So you came into it through the business world. You hired Kim Newton on *Las Vegas*. Did you have something in common?

KIM NEWTON: I was always writing. I wrote for the school newspaper. My dad was a shrink, and my mom had been an English professor. We were always being taken to plays and concerts.

GARDNER: Did your father ever mention cases—"Kimmy, I got this guy who thinks he's an armadillo"?

KIM: He would. His office was in our house. We had this window by the kitchen table, and my brother and I would sit and the patients would walk up and down our driveway. My father would tell their stories, and I would always wonder, as the patients came in and out, "I wonder if that's the guy Dad told me about."

LARRY: Did anybody have a more unusual first work?

LAURIE MCCARTHY: I wrote fortunes for fortune cookies. There was an ad in the *Boston Globe* that offered to pay a dollar for each fortune used. I thought, "How am I going to know if they use it or not?"

LARRY: It's not like there's a residual tracking system for fortunes. So, what did you do to resolve that issue, and what was your favorite fortune?

LAURIE: I got some of those dollars in the mail, which was a shock. And my favorite fortune was, "You will sneeze."

LARRY: So after conquering the world with fortunes, what did you tackle?

LAURIE: I became a copywriter in advertising. Then I moved to New York, and, unlike the rest of the folks here, I decided to actually get my mother's approval on something. So I became an intern on *All My Children* [ABC], which she watched, became a researcher on another show soap, became a writer, and after a couple of years I became a head writer.

LARRY: And your mom said?

LAURIE: "This soap used to be so good. I don't know what happened; it's just boring now."

LARRY: There it is, folks. Don't be in the arts to please someone else. So, in summary, there's much here for aspiring writers to take comfort in. One need not write novels from age six to be considered a writer. Apparently, however, if you can write a spec script at age twelve like Jane, you are some kind of prodigy. Beyond that, however, it doesn't seem to matter what one's first creative attempts may involved. It may be wax candles, songs, poetry, photography, or scripts. The one thing everyone here has in common is that they took those first creative steps, regardless of how the material came out, and they did not get discouraged.

Chapter 7 Lesson

Everyone on our panel was driven by some need to express. What none of them told you, however, was that it took a while to get to the point where they got up the nerve to actually write that first story or poem or script.

You've probably experienced this same thing. You stare at a blank page. You pace. You have this great idea but aren't sure how to start.

You have what we might call "Writer's Block."

You may think that you can blast through it just by jumping into the day's work. But starting this project, or the first writing project of your life, shouldn't be a frivolous event. It requires preparation. If you do not prepare, you will have a hard time making any real headway. And if you don't make headway, you will become discouraged. And if you are discouraged, you will find yourself in despair. And believe me, this point is even more true for experienced writers than rookies.

Despair Not

So, how should you prepare to write? I advise trying a series of writing exercises you may have read about in other books. They take different forms, but they all essentially suggest you sit down and begin writing about something else. Write about anything. Don't think. Just write. Write about what happened to you. Write about the weather. Have two characters named Thing One and Thing Two engage in a dialogue about whatever jumps into your mind. But do not think about any line of dialogue before you write it.

Set an arbitrary minimum limit of twenty minutes, with a maximum of forty minutes. When you are done, seal the envelope up, and put it away. These exercises have provided you with a transition into your personal writing process.

Why? Why go through all this trouble?

A certain philosopher says that we all are in a perpetual state of despair, and most of us don't even know it. The only way to enter a state that is the absence of despair is for "the Self to rest transparently in the spirit which gives it rise," and by doing so, it allows "God to flow through you." I've referred to this state as "The Zone."

In other words, "Feel the Force, Luke. Let go."

So how do we let go, give in to process, let the Self rest transparently within the spirit that gives it rise, or find The Zone? In essence, you have to pray. As a writer, that means working without any kind of plan, just relying on faith. You accomplish that initially through the writing exercises.

In these moments of composition, you are resting transparently within the spirit that gave you rise. You are acting in faith. You are in The Zone. You may begin writing the script.

Other artists utilize different methods. David Lynch dives in the collective subconscious twice a day via transcendental meditation.

If, however, you impose a form or structure to these writing exercises because of some preconceived notion ("I don't want someone to pick this up and read it," "I can't just write gibberish. I need to tell a story," "I'd better produce something today or my wife won't let me be a writer"), then you are not resting transparently in the spirit, and you are in despair. If you are in despair, you will have a hard time being engaged in the process, and your work will suffer for it. You will be more concerned with "writing for the market" or pleasing the showrunner, and that's not going to make your writing all it can be.

What does this task mean psychologically? These exercises train the ego. The ego is that part of us that says, "I am," and it affirms whatever reality it perceives. Thus, if I am not writing, then my ego affirms that I don't write. Even worse, whatever state the ego senses as being in, it extrapolates as a permanent condition. So if I am not writing, then I am not a writer. If I am not a writer, then I never start to write.

Enter procrastination, the hobgoblin of the writer's psyche. You make excuses. "I'm not ready." "I don't know the story well enough yet." "I have to clear my desk before I can concentrate." The insidiousness of it all gets worse because the ego will justify remaining in stasis.

And there you have it—Writer's Block.

So these writing exercises force you to begin. When you are writing, all the things you thought about yourself and the market and the showrunner are gone. Now, when you are going, you don't want to stop. You've performed some jujitsu on the ego. The ego sees you writing, it extrapolates that act to a permanent state, so now you *are* a writer and you don't want to stop. Time to seal up the pages in an envelope and begin the day's real work!

By doing these exercises every day before beginning the script, you are habituating the ego to this behavior. It starts to see writing as essential to your nature.

Back on Planet Earth

Let's examine what our subjects said and see how it jibes with these concepts. In Jason's case, he was actively engaged in journal writing (itself a writing exercise) when he discovered there was something greater within the material. As you might expect, once you reach The Zone, premises for stories are going to come more naturally. Jason appears to have experienced that early on.

Carol, Hart, Jane, Tim, and Vanessa all have something interesting in common. Although their stories don't speak to The Zone directly, they at least heard their spirits telling them to tell a story.

Further Reading

Bernays, Anne, and Pamela Painter. 2003. *What If? Writing Exercises for Fiction Writers*. New York: Longman.

Lynch, David. 2006. *Catching the Big Fish: Meditation, Consciousness, and Creativity*. New York: Tarcher.

8

How to Really Write a Teleplay; or, Why It's about Process, Not Product

Now that you've made it onto the staff of a TV show and have gotten your first episode produced, you will discover a disappointing truth. It seems that all your best lines and scenes have been rewritten. Much of what was "yours" is gone.

In order to keep your morale up, there is yet another fundamental truth about television that you need to learn: process is more important than product. This one may be the second most important "why" you'll read about.

During my tenure at film school, I regarded product as being the ultimate goal of any project. After all, I would spend countless hours slaving away on something so I could see it come to life. I realized my folly when my first produced television episode aired. It was, and remains, my only foray into the world of sitcoms. The show was *Phenom,* produced by the legendary James L. Brooks.

I particularly enjoyed the show's taping. It was like live theater. By this time, my script had been utterly gutted, save for one joke. The story was still intact, but its presentation had changed entirely. This pattern is routine for sitcoms.

Nevertheless, my name appeared under the words *Written by* when the show aired. I got calls from dozens of people congratulating me and telling me how much they liked the show. I realized that I could not launch into the entire story of how the credit was mine, and the story sort of was mine, but that all of the dialogue was different except for this one joke, and so on. I just let it be.

It became apparent that a writer must make a huge number of compromises in order to actually get something produced. The product likely will not resemble the original grand vision, because of the sheer number of hoops the material must jump through to make it to the screen.

That's when it hit me: all my film school professors actually knew what they were talking about. David Lynch, a filmmaker I admire, said it best (I'm paraphrasing): "95 percent of the whole thing is process. It's how you spend all those days. It's life. So you'd better enjoy that part or you aren't enjoying life!"

So, for writers of all stripes, the questions this chapter poses are: What exactly *is* process? Does process differ among writers, or are there commonalities? Must process be entirely intellectual or emotional, or can it contain a mix? If it is a mix, where does one end and the other begin? How do the requirements of television affect one's process?

Finally, why is process important?

Suggested Viewings

Boomtown: "Monster's Brawl," by Javier Grillo-Marxuach
Friday Night Lights: "Eyes Wide Open," by Jason Katims
The Unit: "Two Coins," by David Mamet
Supernatural: "Sin City," by Robert Singer

LARRY: When I first conceived this book, I thought it would be strictly about the writing process. What I did not realize was that process includes everything from birth. So this is the chapter where I'd like everyone to talk about the actual building blocks of outlining and scriptwriting. I slaved over every word on my first scripts because I so wanted to impress my bosses. Gradually, I gained confidence, became less meticulous in my process, and trusted in it more. Bryan, as you wrote that first *Star Trek: Voyager* [1997], were you slaving over every word?

BRYAN FULLER: The more I wrote, the more meticulous I got and the more everything had to be just so.

LARRY: And once you began breaking stories, were you able to let anything personal into those stories, or were you relying solely on craft at that point?

BRYAN: Pretty much on *Star Trek* it was solely craft. There were a couple of episodes that were a little more personal and were better ones. It was tricky because the characters are four hundred years more evolved. They don't speak the way we speak. There was a sterile quality to the dialogue because that's what the genre was. If you tried to venture out of that, you quickly got yanked back in line.

LARRY: The problem with the recent incarnations of *Star Trek* is that the emotion seems to have been pulled out of it.

BRYAN: Completely. It's all intellectual ideas.

LARRY: What always amazed me was the fact that those shows were so successful given the lack of emotional contact.

BRYAN: The plots move forward based on incident or intellect, but rarely dependent on whether a character was feeling something relatable. One of the episodes I did, "Barge of the Dead" [1999], had an atheist who had an experience that made him believe in the afterlife, and he throws his whole belief system out the window. He did not know what to believe anymore, and that was something that was very relatable and emotional: "If what I'm experiencing is real to me, doesn't that make it real?" And that was a much more satisfying story to write.

LARRY: In relying strictly on an intellectual approach, were you able to write something that you did not believe in yourself?

BRYAN: Yes, because in the *Star Trek* context you have to believe in the logic of the story. It's a much more Vulcan take on storytelling.

LARRY: What is your actual writing process?

BRYAN: I put earplugs in. I have to work in absolute quiet. The noisier and more active the environment is, the harder it is for me to work. I will do whatever it takes to get into the vibe and start thinking about a scene in a different way. Chances are I'm writing a scene that I've seen before, dramatically speaking. I need to use them not as buoys to swim to but orange cones to go around, so I can find unique ways to tell that scene again.

LARRY: So how do you?

BRYAN: I turn the emotion on, or play a different emotional angle on how the character is trying to get their objective. Far too often in scripts, people say what they think. Yet, in real life, I bite my tongue because if I said what I think I wouldn't have any friends.

LARRY: Chris, in the actual scene construction, do you find that you start at the beginning and go straight through?

CHRIS BRANCATO: I'll come into a scene and know exactly what the ending is, so I'll write the end and I'll write it backwards up to the top. Other times, I know the beginning, and I'll pop in there. It's almost like a canvas in the rough-draft stage.

LARRY: Michael, in the writing process of your early years, did you slave over every line?

MICHAEL CHERNUCHIN: Every word.

LARRY: And once done did you find you had something pretty solid, or did it still need much rewriting?

MICHAEL: It's all about rewriting. That's the whole process. I spend each day rereading what I did yesterday, marking it up and changing it.

LARRY: Do you generate stories from personal emotional moments or high-concept intellectual places? On *Law & Order* your bible was the *New York Post*, no?

MICHAEL: Yes, but not straight re-creations, because it's boring. So we took the story and made it go someplace else.

LARRY: So taking a high-concept story, was there something personal that you added to each story?

MICHAEL: Always.

LARRY: Is that a requirement for your process, that you must have a vested emotional interest in what you're writing, or can you just rely on craft if need be? Could you produce a great script that way?

MICHAEL: I could fake it, write clever dialogue, jokes and things like that, which are also personal. Again, it's not about me, but something I care about or have thought about much. I always try to elevate it even if on a deadline.

LARRY: I think every television writer faces a major pitfall in every episode, and that is the repetition of scenes. That is, the scene isn't a direct copy of what came before, but that certain beats are repeated and the story does not move forward.

MICHAEL: Repetition is a big problem. In fact, if you step back and look at *Law & Order* it's all just talking heads. So you must make it feel like it's moving forward by jumping into a scene as late as possible and getting out quickly.

LARRY: Scorsese always says that. Parachute into a scene.

MICHAEL: And repetition will also tip you off that the author doesn't really have anything to say.

LARRY: Do you personally have a political agenda in your stories?

MICHAEL: No, I fight against it. You can watch every episode of *Law & Order,* and you won't know what my politics are. The fun part of the show is writing both sides, such as why there should or should not be a death penalty. That's where you must stretch. Find a reason that opposes your own beliefs.

LARRY: How has your writing process changed over fourteen years working in TV?

MICHAEL: I'm much more confident now and don't struggle as much. At first, I feared the same thing about every script: "Are they going to throw it out?"

LARRY: Do you prefer large blocks of time to write?

MICHAEL: The only time I can is when we're shut down in New York, yet some of my best stuff comes at 3:00 a.m.

LARRY: It's like you get out of the office and take a drive, and you decompress from the script problem—

MICHAEL: And the answer comes to you. And you get up in the morning, and you put it down. Many people can get screwed if you don't fix the problem, so fear is a great motivator.

LARRY: What's your writing process, Tim?

TIM KRING: I write a really detailed outline for myself because when I write a script, I then only focus on the scene itself and not where I'm going or where I've been. I've done all that work earlier, and it all makes sense.

LARRY: Do you begin at the beginning of a scene and just find your way through it?

TIM: I'll just start having people talk.

LARRY: Do you feel your scenes are fairly complete because of being so detailed in your outline? Do you go back and revise?

TIM: I can't go forward until it's done. I'm very anal retentive that way, and if I can't get it right, I'll just drop anchor and stay there until I get it right. Some scenes just take forever, and others are done instantly.

LARRY: So by the time you're done with a first draft—

TIM: A first draft to me is a very complete draft.

LARRY: So how does the staff of *Las Vegas* work in terms of composing scenes?

GARDNER STERN: I go from the beginning straight through to the end.

LARRY: Editing as you go?

GARDNER: I write on a yellow legal pad. I'm a bad typist, and I can get it down faster when some thought comes into my head, but then I'll scratch stuff out, have arrows pointing all over the place. I don't think, "Oh, here's the line that should end the scene," and start with that. I think that's a bad way to write. It puts you in a network mind-set, where they're always asking, "What's the button on the scene?" It makes all this stuff very homogenous.

KIM NEWTON: If I end on page 15 today, then tomorrow I'll backtrack to rework things. I tend to just make passes over drafts. I'm more of a first-draft girl than a rewrite girl. I don't really enjoy rewriting as much as I enjoy the first draft.

LARRY: And do you find that your first drafts are complete because you've really massaged a scene before you move on to the next one?

KIM: I feel like they're more instinctual. Things get homogenized when you have six people's notes going and you're trying to make them all work. Then you have something that maybe you did not even want, to address all those notes, and it becomes less yours.

LARRY: So make that first draft really yours.

KIM: It's the easiest way to live with it. The first draft is not necessarily the best draft, but at least it's yours.

GARDNER: Writing the first draft is definitely the part I enjoy most. I'm just doing what I think is good.

LARRY: Do you improvise out loud? Is that a process you use? Are the voices coming to your head?

KIM: I sort of play out the roles as I'm typing. I don't act them out physically, but I have them in my head, and I'll say stuff out loud at home, but not here. I like to see how it rolls off the tongue, if it's too long, or too complicated. If it has anything to do with comedy, I can't trust just reading it; I have to say it out loud to see if there's a rhythm and see how it would actually play.

GARDNER: I envision the scene in my head, so I hear in my head all the different characters talking. It helps if you are familiar with them and you know how they'll say a certain line. Like Kim, after I write it on a yellow piece of paper, I dictate it to my assistant, and that's almost like another draft. As I hear the words come out, something won't sound right, and I'll just change it.

LARRY: Medicine is all about storytelling, isn't it, Neal?

NEAL BAER: The best doctors are good storytellers. They know how to convey the patient's story to other physicians so that they can come to a diagnosis. That's really the art of medicine. One must do a presentation that's dramatic, that should have a beginning and an end, and should leave some point for the people to ask for the other doctor's frankness. People are listening, and they're engaged because these are true stories about people's lives.

LARRY: Neal, you mentioned mythology as being a big love of yours. I love Joseph Campbell and agree with his assertion that we tell stories as a way of finding meaning.

NEAL: It's also how we communicate. I teach at USC and ask my students, when I first meet them, to think if they have spoken to anyone that day, and if so, did they tell a story? They all say yes, except the ones who have just arrived from waking up. The point is that the currency of our lives is stories. What did you do yesterday? What happened last night? We don't just talk to each other. In fact, there's a structure, there's a beginning and an end. If you can't pull it together, you're autistic, or something is typically wrong with you. So when I write, I always ask, "Is it a good story?" I never think about the audience. I figure if it's a good story, and it's suited me well so far, and I find it compelling and can relate to it, if it raises questions I don't know the answers to, then maybe other people will feel the same way.

LARRY: Shawn, do you write straight through and revise or slog through scene by scene?

SHAWN RYAN: I write the whole thing first, and then I'll revise.

LARRY: David Mamet joined the ranks of TV writers with *The Unit*. What's his approach?

SHAWN: David has a different perspective. He is about characterization and behavior. He also explicates the difference between obstacles and situations. Situations are preexisting conditions that these people are in that they talk about. He's not interested in those. He's interested in the *obstacle* in this particular episode that needs to be overcome. What does that person do? And then what are we, as the audience, supposed to bring to this character by watching him handle, overcome, not overcome, succeed, or get defeated by that obstacle?

LARRY: Dan, does your acting experience play into your writing?

DAN BUCATINSKY: I let myself write out a scene, and I improvise it exactly as you said. I was in an improv group in New York ten years ago. It was 100 percent improvised. The person who would step out onto that stage and you would step out with them, and you would literally be hanging by a thread waiting to hear what they were going to say next. The scene would literally materialize before you. I admire that because it truly is what writing is about. As I improvise, I decide I want to see a character do X, Y, or Z. Then I work backwards.

LARRY: Give us an example.

DAN: A guy picks up the wrong piece of luggage at the baggage carousel, he gets into a cab, and he winds up in a restaurant. No, he winds up actually where dogs sniff out firearms. And he has to prove who he is. So, how did that happen? So, I work backwards. I need to know why he is on the plane. Who is he talking to on the plane? What is that conversation like? And then I try to imitate real life. I think about when I was on an airplane and what that sounded like. If I can create authenticity to that guy, when he asks for that second round of peanuts on the plane, we will understand why he does.

LARRY: So what would you say is the purpose of improv?

DAN: It's all about energy. Keeping it up. Not giving yourself time to think, because if you do, you're toast. So apply that to writing. Find the scene objective and just start writing. You have to be so dependent on the moment and so completely clear. And the only way to do that is to not know what the next line is.

LARRY: Aaron and Gretchen, what about when you're writing as a team?

AARON HARBERTS: When I'm writing I *am* the character. I'm writing things that I might not necessarily believe. I literally put myself in that character's shoes and express what that *character* would say.

LARRY: So that's your acting experience coming into play, isn't it?

AARON: I don't know. When I'm actually in The Zone, I'm not thinking about anything. I might be thinking about rhythm, or what the right word might be. But I never dictate that this is what the character must say. I always come from what the character is.

LARRY: So that's picking up a little of what Dan was saying. Some writers channel themselves into the character, on a conscious level.

GRETCHEN BERG: It's hard for me to do. For all the characters that we've written or created, to have them all share my point of view would be so boring, I can't imagine. Part of creating characters is they are outside of you, and what's fun is to walk in someone else's shoes. If I want to push some agenda, I'd talk to a friend on the phone. But as far as using the characters to say what I need said, isn't that what therapy's for?

LARRY: For some writers the two are one and the same! And on the studio's dime! Let's turn to outlines versus actual scriptwriting. I can write a twelve-page outline with lots of detail, and then the script will come out very quickly. However, I prefer to work from a simple beat sheet so as to allow discovery within the scene. I feel it is more creative and much more energetic that way. In fact, if I can work without even a beat sheet, I'm happiest. How do you do it, Javier?

JAVIER GRILLO-MARXUACH: I do my writing for myself that way. Most of my series writing, though, requires outlines. On *Lost* outlines are twenty-six to thirty-two pages.

LARRY: That's unusually long.

JAVIER: They're not in script format, but they have dialogue. We go through everything, beat by beat. That's the way that Damon Lindelof likes to work.

LARRY: You were on *Boomtown* with Chris. For readers who haven't seen the show, it told a story from multiple points of view, and was nonlinear.

JAVIER: That's the show that took my Writers' Room skills to really the next level.

LARRY: Were those stories broken individually?

JAVIER: Sort of. Graham Yost could figure out that show internally. I remember him pitching one episode that he just figured out in his mind, in nonlinear structure. He put it up on the board, and it was this beautiful poetic piece of nonlinear writing, and we all felt, "How the hell do we measure up to that?" First we were trying to break the show the way that Graham did it, and that did not work. Then we were trying to break the stories individually and put them back together. And that did not quite work. And there were one or two other ways that we tried to skin that cat. Then we decided to break the entire story from the beginning, middle, and end. And then finally, we collectively came to this idea that we weren't doing it right because we weren't *conceptually* doing it right. What we had to figure out was to tell three short stories about the characters. And once we figured those out, with a beginning, middle, and an end, we assembled them for the show. Once we did that, we had a real breakthrough. We had a method. The fact that it took us a while to figure out how to do it made us a really good unit, in terms of working in The Room.

LARRY: Chris, you want to jump in on this?

CHRIS: We knew we had to come up with a log-line that was coherent, simple, and compelling and then come up with the different characters and viewpoints. Then Graham would often fly into an outline that would be too long and unproducible for television. My partner, Bert, and I were there to tell him, "That's absolutely crazy."

LARRY: What about the order in which those viewpoints were presented?

CHRIS: To be honest, I found we could somewhat arbitrarily interchange the viewpoints. Still, to write the perfect *Boomtown* script each perspective would give us a little bit more information so that you could not switch them around.

LARRY: A purist might say, "What's special about the show if you can just interchange things?" Was there a side of you that said, "It's bullshit if we can move it around like that"?

CHRIS: No, not at all. First of all, with the writing process, you often move things around, regardless of whether it's a traditional structure or a *Boomtown*. Then also in the editing room, when you're actually making television, you're always rewriting that too.

LARRY: Excellent point. Javier, can a writer survive only on craft?

JAVIER: There are writers whom I admire exclusively for their craft that don't have the amount of insight or vision that I prefer. However, I know that if I were running a show, I could hand them an outline, and I'd get a script that I could shoot. And that's worth its weight in gold. 'Cause you can have the most poetic, wise human being on your staff, but if they can't crank out sixty pages in five days, they're no good.

LARRY: So when all else fails, you have craft.

JAVIER: Everybody ultimately finds their greatest level of ability by mastering the craft. You may be a great writer of emotion, but the craft is what allows you to express what you have to express in the way that you need to express it. The language of writing is the craft of creating a script that works as a script and is a work of art in and of itself that somebody can read and understand intuitively. That's one of the things that annoy me most about many books on writing. They say a script is really a blueprint for a picture. If a script is not a readable work of art with a narrative that propels the readers through the page in a meaningful way and that provides its own emotional journey, you've failed.

LARRY: Akira Kurosuwa said at the 1990 Academy Awards when he got a special award, "Thank you very much. I promise to keep learning."

JAVIER: You must have a healthy level of humility about writing itself. You always have to learn. That's what I see as the downfall of many writers. They get so comfortable with what their strengths are that they never figure out how to go beyond that.

LARRY: And the money's too good.

JAVIER: I've always worked with people who've been very challenging in terms of what they wanted out of me. I can't say I've left my
ego behind, but I've left my need to be the smartest guy in the room
behind. And I've realized that if I'm the smartest guy in the room, I'm
in trouble. When I was in my early twenties, negative criticism got to
me in a very visceral way.

LARRY: It's hard not to let it.

JAVIER: But I've come to the conclusion that there is nobody who can tell
me that I'm a bad writer. I may not be doing the type of writing they
want me to do, but I know that my craft is solid. Security in the craft is
what makes it possible for you to be daring in the creativity.

LARRY: And yet there are those moments where even craft can get you
twisted up.

JAVIER: You have to stay very strict in the confines of a franchise so that
new viewers always know what the show is about. That was the case
with me as a story editor on *The Pretender*. The things that I found
difficult about that show were the formula aspects of it. I remember
writing that bomb-squad episode where I had literally prostrated
myself facedown on the floor of my office, saying, "I'm never going
to work again." So I walk out of my office, and there's co–executive
producer Tommy Thompson sitting there. He says, "What's going on?
You don't look good." I fly into this monologue: "I'm having a really
terrible problem because Jarod is in the bomb squad, and they get a
bomb in a hotel, and I have him in the office. How are they going to
get from the office to the hotel? Do they get the threat in the office?
Do they get in the car? Do I show them driving the car? Or are they
sitting in the car—are they driving the car to the hotel?" And Tommy
just listened and said, "Show them getting the threat, and then cut to
them, running into the hotel." And I said, "You're a genius!" And I ran
back in my office.

LARRY: You can get too wrapped up in the trees to see the forest.

JAVIER: The thing that made it difficult was that the formula was so in the
DNA of the show that, in that first season, it led to a creative paralysis.
I felt that if it hadn't been done before in some way, in the show, then
I did not feel like I had permission to do it. And the sad thing was

that was a self-imposed thing. It was a really valuable lesson because I learned to just say to myself, "You have to give yourself permission to write what you're going to write. You have to give yourself the freedom to find those spaces where you put yourself into the script." Ultimately, you and I wrote an episode together; it was a story where *The Pretender* stuff is very small, and instead we had many emotional things in it. It was a moment when it was the great fusion of concepts and formula, because that episode was no different from any of the other *Pretender* episodes. It was just one where, in writing it, you and I were able to hit on some things that really resonated, and it made for a really great episode. So when you're in a show, you got a formula, but your job as a writer is to figure out how to put yourself into the formula and help with the humanity.

LARRY: Javier hit on one writer's obstacle. Hart, what happens if you really get stuck on something when you're writing?

HART HANSON: I go back to theme or find the tangible thing that the protagonist wants. The next layer is to ask why they want that thing, and that's usually the theme.

LARRY: How do you handle story structure?

HART: I plot the A-, B-, and C-stories separately. That way each individual story works, and I do a melded outline from that.

LARRY: Do you work from detailed outlines?

HART: Always, but only twelve pages for an hour show.

LARRY: How much of the specifics of a scene do you want in the outline?

HART: When it's just for me, I'll note important plot points. I actually have a table showing these points in my writing program.

LARRY: How do you approach a scene?

HART: I write much, starting from the beginning. I write it over and over and over. I get to the point where I have everything I need in a scene, and then move on to polish it later. I would never show anyone my first draft. They'd think I was retarded.

LARRY: Do you actually hear voices in your head, and walk around the room talking to yourself as you compose?

HART: No. I do a pass that is not in the character's voice, then another pass to put it into their syntax.

LARRY: Laurie, where do you come down on this?

LAURIE MCCARTHY: Depends on the situation. Because such a great part of television is trying to get things through the approval process and not go backward.

LARRY: Let's talk idealistically then.

LAURIE: I'm fifty-fifty. I've done it both ways, and sometimes I like to not have it broken down at all. I've written a number of procedurals, and I find that a detailed outline really helps, or you can just spin off in the worst possible way. It might be interesting, but it's not going to solve your case.

LARRY: What was your approach to writing for *CSI*? Crime is a weird thing because coming up with a cool case is very intellectual. Did you base stories on something real?

LAURIE: I chose things I always thought would be scary or wanted to explore, but the ramifications of which would be far-reaching. Once you find a story, you can't help but view it with compassion and humanity.

LARRY: So how do you approach writing a criminal? They've done something which you can't fathom doing.

LAURIE: To me the best crime stories explain how a person came to that point in their life.

LARRY: They're always very relatable, aren't they?

LAURIE: They're very relatable and often quite inevitable.

LARRY: Crimes of passion.

LAURIE: Crimes of passion where it's not a big surprise when the gun went off, despite it being a personal tragedy.

LARRY: And you find that humanity in the criminal, too.

LAURIE: I think that's the first place I find it. A crime is always a story told backwards. So you want to make sure that if you told that story linearly, it's interesting and engaging. And I think that's following the criminal's train of thought.

LARRY: When you're writing a scene, do you walk around the room and talk to yourself?

LAURIE: I did not think that I talked to myself when writing scenes, but my assistant told me that I do. And I've been doing it at the computer.

And sometimes when I think now that I've become aware that I'm doing it, I find that I won't do it, or I'll have written it down and read it aloud.

LARRY: Do you write a quick draft, then go back and revise?

LAURIE: I've noticed two kinds of people. One does stream of consciousness to the end, and then loops back. I tend to edit as I go, one step forward, one step back even within a scene, unless it's something that really flows out of you that just naturally leads you to a structure. But there's usually so much story to accomplish in a scene, and there are a number of story elements that need to be platformed, so I find that those are where I start out.

LARRY: Do you slave over every word?

LAURIE: I'm really critical of myself as I go, but the slaving over every word happens on a final picky pass where I do things like make sure I did not use a word too many times. And I pull out words I just don't like. I can't stand the word *it*, for example.

LARRY: And besides the picky pass, once you've actually written a scene, what percentage stays intact to your final draft?

LAURIE: About 70 percent of that usually winds up on-air. I'm pretty brutal as I go.

LARRY: In your experience, are you able to articulate differences between the male and the female creative process?

LAURIE: I haven't really noticed a difference, actually. But in The Room I see some disparity. In general, I think women tend to edit themselves more, and are culturally taught to be more deferential and more apologetic about their opinion. Men are more comfortable being declarative—owning a pitch, as it were.

LARRY: Have you picked up any bad habits writing for television, Vanessa?

VANESSA TAYLOR: I talked to showrunner Greg Berlanti about a feature I'm working on. And his note was, "You've become so accustomed to writing quickly that you haven't stopped to think if the way you've written a scene is the best way." And he was right. I became so used to writing quickly that I did not even stop to think.

LARRY: Frank, what's the most critical part of the writing process for you?

FRANK MILITARY: Point of view is everything. Sex, religion, God, politics, love, race, friendship, sports, poker.

LARRY: That also sounds like an actor talking. When you go into a scene, you have to have an attitude, a point of view, and you have to make choices as well. Is that something you think came from acting that might have slopped over, or did you learn that independently?

FRANK: I don't know which came first, the chicken or the egg. I'm always surprised when I see actors that don't have the tools to analyze a script. Instinctually, they know that there's a problem, but nine times out of ten they blame it on themselves. I have friends who audition, and I'll work with them and say, "You're completely fulfilling what this is. The problem is in the page. It's not a problem of you getting into a certain head space of where this character is or an emotional space of where this character is. It's not that. You're doing it. It's just not there on the page."

LARRY: I always do a pass where I put on the actor's hat and remind myself: "What's the objective for the actor? How are they going to play this? What is the intention behind this line?" I feel like it adds an extra foundation for the script. Is that something you're doing instinctually because of your training?

FRANK: All of us have the actor's voice in our heads because we sit and read our work. And we don't read it at reading speed; we read it at the pace and rhythm of the scene, and that's us acting. We should all listen to a read-through, listen to actors' comments.

LARRY: So do you work from outlines?

FRANK: Yes, extremely detailed ones. There was a feature project I did years ago, and I pitched a very detailed pitch, got the job, and was told to go write it. I did not do a detailed outline. When the script was handed in somebody said, "This was not what we bought." It *was* what they bought, but I did not have an outline to prove it. Getting notes in essence becomes a contract between you and the entity you're working for. I was very young, and it upset me; I thought it was slander.

LARRY: What do you tell people who hate to outline?

FRANK: When I speak with younger writers, they fight structure. Yet look at simply structured music, like the blues. When people are beginning to improvise they use the structure because it is freeing. A well-structured story is usually embodied through a well-structured outline. It gives me the most creative and fun moment in the writing process. When the outline is done, I know where the train is going. I can put on music now and disappear in an almost meditative way into the actual writing. Blues is great for learning, but if you go to jazz and you begin to understand more progressions, you know where you're going, and you're free to take the composition and find your unique direction.

LARRY: Does writing scare you?

FRANK: The diving in is frightening for all writers until the moment that they dive in. And that's the great thing. I know many, many writers that are filled with anxiety about their profession. I don't have anxiety when I'm working, because I'm putting my butt in the chair and doing everything I can to make the project as good as it should be, and that's all I can do.

LARRY: Do you work on a scene until it's done and you can move on, like Tim?

FRANK: The scenes I go over are the ones that give me pleasure. I choose to sit and amuse myself. I want to get to the end and read a first draft. There will be lots of problems, but the big question that must have been answered is: "Is this working? Is this structure working— are these themes coming through?" That's what I'm nervous about, because if those aren't working, the rest of it is irrelevant.

LARRY: It's the world of pragmatism versus our idealistic selves as writers. Do you believe there is such a thing as writer's block, or do you believe it is just an excuse for insecurity?

FRANK: A friend of mine was asking that same question. I said, "I've never had writer's block." And she said, "Oh, Frank, now you're acting like an idiot." I said, "No, part of the reason is I'm a screenwriter. I only have a few things I have to actually focus on each year. So I was never blocked in the sense of there being a blank sheet of paper." There's so much process that I can do mechanically, and so little I need to produce.

LARRY: I don't think anybody really does have writer's block, and that's why I'm trying to figure out what it really is. I believe it is insecurity.

FRANK: There's that natural reluctance that we have to start on something. Many nonwriters get insecure, they move forward, and they
stop. The metaphor I use is if you were an explorer crossing the Atlantic and you get into a boat for the first time. If Europe is three weeks
behind you, and you don't know what the hell is in front of you, then
you'd be scared on that boat. But if you made that crossing twelve
times, you'd be bored to tears, but you'd be confident. That's the difference between a professional and an amateur writer. Pros have the
confidence to wake up and say, "We're lost today. Next time when
we're lost we go back to research, we write a character, we reread
the book, we reread the magazine article, we call our friends and go
have lunch." Amateurs get knocked back, they tend to stop, and the
project follows.

LARRY: Jane, what's your process for breaking story and writing the
script?

JANE ESPENSON: I've never figured myself as a good story breaker. I
think because it's so abstract, I don't have my hands on it. With fingers
on the keyboard, it just sort of becomes complete. And I don't care if I
get good at the story until I'm actually writing the outline.

LARRY: So for you that process requires something tangible, something
you can work out yourself.

JANE: When I'm alone looking at the keyboard, and words on a screen,
it's real. When it's people talking, I found that really hard. It's like you
said, it's intangible, it's—

LARRY: Not as secure creatively?

JANE: Maybe. I am still very much about pleasing the showrunner, and
for me that comes at the computer rather than in The Room.

LARRY: So you prefer detailed outlines, with specificity.

JANE: Not too much. I like making it come alive by finding special little
beats at the keyboard.

LARRY: How do you approach a scene?

JANE: I'm all over the place. I write out of order. I write the scenes I have
most clearly visualized. I write little chunks of scenes before the
whole thing.

LARRY: So you write nonlinearly. What happens after that first draft?

JANE: It used to be that I hated it when I wrote it, but once I'd read it, it stuck. And now I'm getting better at saying, "Nope, that's not what I wanted from the scene. Throw it out. Start over."

LARRY: I think that's really common. There's this tendency to want to believe something is better than it is so we can just move on, or perhaps avoid having to fix what we know is bad yet don't know how to fix.

JANE: I've learned that I have to be careful not to write too early, to really visualize it well first, because otherwise it'll get written badly, and then I won't have the impetus to change it.

LARRY: Bob, do you work linearly? You mentioned that you start with your act-outs first, but once you have those, do you track beginning to end?

ROBERT SINGER: Yeah, but I have a long kind of germination period, where I just walk around. I try to find the characters' voices. I write these scenes in my head, and they stay there. They change, but I come back to them; I use them. Sometimes I use them as guideposts.

LARRY: Are these plot-driven moments, or character moments?

ROBERT: The latter. Then I start feeling comfortable with whom the people are. Then it's easier for me to go. I'll just start with a line. There's one line in every scene for me, and the scene goes off from that.

LARRY: A line that's critical to the scene?

ROBERT: Usually. Sometimes that line ends up coming in the first thing in the scene, or it's the last line in the scene.

LARRY: Robert Zemeckis called that "the red dot." It encapsulates what's going on not only within the scene but also sometimes thematically with the script—if you're lucky.

ROBERT: That'd be great. I would imagine if you took that line or that one exchange from each scene, and just took each scene and did those lines, you'd get a pretty good idea of what the show was about. And who the characters are.

Chapter 8 Lesson

Once you are writing for television, you may have a real struggle on your hands because the demands of television appear to impact the ability to produce truth in drama.

How can we find the truth in a script when the script is due the next day? If we aren't in The Zone, then we are in despair. If we are in despair, then our work is false. Some writers, myself included, believe that outlines are an expression of despair because you aren't really writing. You are playing it safe, giving yourself a road map, and there are no maps when one is resting transparently. The ego is controlling us in these moments, and if we are not writing, then we are not writers at that moment.

But how does this jibe with Michael Chernuchin's statement that solutions often come to him when he gets away from the desk? I've had countless incidences of inspiration when I'm not writing. Does that mean that my subconscious delivers answers? Does that mean that my subconscious may be in The Zone when I'm taking a walk in the park?

Besides, Frank Military likes to work from a very detailed outline. It frees him to enter the actual writing of the scene without having to analyze his characters' actions, to "disappear in a meditative way into the actual writing." He knows what his characters must accomplish, so he is free to improvise. He is thus able to trust in his process and know that the material he produces will be organic. In this case, then, I don't see how the outline can be labeled an expression of despair.

Everyone has a personal way of approaching the writing process. Of particular fascination, however, is that process rarely seems to be exclusively derived from one thing at any one time. Although some writers do focus exclusively on emotion at one moment, most seem to be constantly multitasking. The actual process of writing—the actual *in-the-moment process*—is this magical nexus of intellect, emotion, craft, and experience. Is this juncture The Zone, or is it just a mishmash of craft thrown together to get the script finished and actually an expression of despair?

What are we to make of all these contradictions and definitions?

Well, too much knowledge can be a bad thing. Let's back off and try to sort it out.

The Zone in Restraints?

Yes, television imposes restrictions on us. Yes, we must serve the vision of a showrunner, grapple with the vagaries of the studio, and deal with the censorship of Standards & Practices. But nothing—nothing—prevents us from resting transparently in the spirit that gives us rise when we are writing, regardless of what we are writing. If you aren't in The Zone, it's your own fault. Take responsibility.

It doesn't matter what the show is. What matters is what you bring to the process of writing it.

Look at *Friday Night Lights*. This show is about the lives of teenagers and parents at a Texas high school. I doubt I've seen any scene from this show that has not been done countless times elsewhere. However, the confluence of all the elements in each episode (of which the writing is paramount) creates something where nothing was before. The scenes resonate in spite of themselves. Suddenly, the characters of a television show become living, breathing people I care deeply for. Why? How? Because the show was written in The Zone. That fact is to the great credit of not only Jason Katims and his staff of writers but also the astonishing talent of his young cast and the brilliant idea to shoot in a faux-documentary style. *Every artist*, not just the writers, was clearly in The Zone at every stage of the process.

Back to Acting

For writers who still doubt the usefulness of acting classes, this chapter may convince them to reconsider. As Frank Military says, "All of us have the actor's voice in our heads because we sit and read our work. And we don't read it at reading speed; we read it at the pace and rhythm of the scene, and that's us acting." Furthermore, Frank told us that "point of view is everything." It's true of writing, and it's true of acting.

Having come from the actor's world, Frank prepared himself to be a writer without ever realizing it. Of all the arts, acting may be the most frightening. It requires you to stand up in front of a group of strangers, to do and say the most outrageous and potentially embarrassing things, and in the process elicit emotion from the audience. But that performance, in and of itself, is not what causes fear. *Thinking* causes fear and anxiety, by stepping outside of yourself and recognizing reality for what it is: extended moments of total vulnerability to an audience. It is these thoughts—the ones that are self-critical and therefore an expression of despair—that cripple the artist. Thought leads to analysis, which causes the rational mind to consider the possibility of failure. Frank Military became a successful actor because of his ability to sweep the thought aside. The same is true as to how he became a successful writer.

He understood how he reached The Zone.

The very best actors, and consequently the very best writers, remove the critical voices from their heads before and during their creative process. Frank immerses himself in his character as part of his acting process. He develops and internalizes his character's point of view about every aspect of life. He focuses on the character's objective in a scene. When the scene begins, he uses the writer's words to guide his character toward that goal. Ideally, he becomes so immersed in this process that he does not have the opportunity to step outside of his character and *think*. That's his Nirvana.

Remember, improvisational actors are taught to avoid thought. They are taught to just make a choice in the moment and run with it. They are taught to say yes to every single possibility, so that *action is guaranteed*. So, too, must the writer avoid too much thought. Yes, a certain amount is required in formulating a story, and thought is essential when analyzing a completed scene or script in order to improve it. But don't let it drive you as you write.

Actors Have a Zone, Too

In television, the continual exploration and development of the characters over many episodes augment this process. As each actor interprets the writer's words and adds special touches (from achieving The Zone), the writer discovers shadings to the character that did not exist before and builds on them in the next script.

In the grandest of creative accomplishments, the showrunner's vision melds with the writers' scripts and the actors' interpretations to form a truly living being—a separate entity that exists independently of its creators. Something has been created where nothing was before.

If we, the writers, are lucky, there is one final achievement in the process. The character—this ethereal being—begins to dictate actions to the writers. As we have inhabited them, so they have inhabited us.

Michael Chernuchin's experience with actors also demonstrates a fundamental truth about writing for television. Somebody will always have a different interpretation of the words set on the page. In Hollywood, or on the stage, a power struggle may commence over the best way to interpret that material. These moments can be frustrating and maddening. However, if all artists are devoted to making the Work as a whole come alive (take the "me" out of it), it can be tremendously rewarding.

As writers, we live in our heads as we compose. Upon completion, it exists in a vacuum of perfection. But when it is given to actors, it will mutate into an entirely new life form. Perhaps it will be 100 percent reflective of the intent and vision of the author. Perhaps it will be different, but different does not mean it will be better or worse. It will simply be what came next.

The other lesson here is that the Work is never truly complete, because it will always be taken from the writer's hands at some point. And therein lies the eternal dilemma of the writer: to release a personal vision to the hearts and minds of the audience—who come to the material with their own set of experiences. It will once again transform into something different as they experience it, and transform yet again when they process it.

The television business is about compromise, but so is life. You rarely get your way all the time. As a writer, all you can do is take the material as far as time or sanity will allow and then send it out into the world, satisfied that you have accomplished everything you wanted to with the Work. For beyond that point lies the chaotic universe, over which you have no control.

Process is more important than product, because the product is both transitory and subject to interpretation. But process is about you. It's yours. You own it. Enjoy it.

Further Reading

Goldberg, Natalie. 2005. *Writing Down the Bones: Freeing the Writer Within.* New York: Shambala.

9

How to Run a Show; or, Why You Should Be Careful What You Wish For

It's more than just the brass ring. It's the top of the world. Your own show. Your own vision. Your writing staff. Your final word. You can do whatever you want: push people around, tell executives to get stuffed, decide what the best stories are and what the voices of the characters are, make decisions about everything that matters to you, rewrite everyone and take screen credit, and tell stories that will change the world!

Right?

Suggested Viewings

Six Feet Under: "Can I Come Up Now?" by Alan Ball
The West Wing: "Enemies Foreign and Domestic," by Paul Redford and Aaron Sorkin
The Sopranos: "Employee of the Month," by Robin Green and Mitchell Burgess

LARRY: There are so many aspects of showrunning to cover, but because this is a discussion mostly about writing, let's start there. Bob, you have the most experience here, I think. We talked about writers bringing something they care about to a piece. Sometimes, they put their heart and soul into it. Do you find yourself needing to be sensitive to that? And what about you? Is there value in helping them keep their desired emotional core to a piece?

ROBERT SINGER: If you don't have an emotional investment in the script you're working on, then what's the point? At the same time, though, the writer knows it doesn't have to be Shakespeare. Brandon Tartikoff's greatest gift was that he'd get as excited about *Alf* as he would about *Hill Street Blues*. So you can't second-guess the audience. If you're always looking back, you're going to be derivative.

LARRY: There is no way to predict success, so the only thing we can rely on is what moves us. But as the middleman between writer and network, do you feel you must tune in to what this writer wants to say?

ROBERT: Well, the writer had that themselves. But when you work with a really good writer, you've got to not be a martinet. Barbara Turner would never let you be a martinet because she's as tough as nails. She has a vision that's her own and unique. Working with a good writer like her has really serviced me over the years for running shows. Some people tell me I'm crazy, but if it comes down to what I want and what the writer has written and it's really just different—not better—then I'm always going to leave it alone.

LARRY: Let the writer express.

ROBERT: I want the writer invested in the show. If a writer feels the script's going to come to my desk and there won't be anything left of it, then he can just hand in gibberish because he'll think I'm going to change it anyway. I like them to be invested. I like them to feel they have a shot, as many shots as far as time allows. I never want them walking away feeling, "I did not get my chance." Now sometimes late in the year you can't help that, because the time crunch is what it is.

LARRY: But a pro will understand that.

ROBERT: Yeah. I've never really had a writer get mad at me for changing stuff. And I think it's just because of the way I go about my business. The door is always open. And it is collaborative, certainly until the eleventh hour.

LARRY: Your demeanor, and rep, is that you are a very straightforward guy.

ROBERT: An exec at NBC said, "Your shows are either the best to work on or the worst to work on." And I said, "Why?" He said, "Well, you have more respect for other writers than most guys. You give them their head way more than most guys. But the guillotine is not far away if you don't like what they're doing."

LARRY: What are other necessary qualities for a showrunner?

ROBERT: You must have a broad vision and be able to know what your strength is. Play to it. Then hire people and let them do their job. A showrunner who gets hung up in the editing room for five hours a day is wasting his time. Get a great postproduction person. Phil Sgriccia has been with me for years and gets those cuts to a good place.

LARRY: Which makes your job easier.

ROBERT: I'll spend two hours in there, and then another hour and a half the next time they bring it back through, reflecting my changes. But that's all. You must trust those people that you hire. You must trust that number-two person on the staff that they can do rewriting, so that by the time it gets to me, that script has been through a process. I had a young staff writer on a show named Liz Friedman. I put her through hell on one of her shows, and she thanked me for it later. That script that we shot was her script.

LARRY: Bob, I've worked with great showrunners and nutcases. The people here have worked on successful shows and disasters. So, which showrunners fail and why?

ROBERT: The biggest fault is they get there too fast. I had worked a long time before I started running shows. The executive producer really has to be perceived as the boss. Everything has to have their imprimatur on it.

LARRY: I feel like ego can be a big problem.

ROBERT: That's the worst thing to have in the job. I mean, everybody needs a healthy ego. But your writers need a healthy ego, too.

LARRY: It seems there are some people, like you, who run a tight ship, and others who just seem to thrive on chaos.

ROBERT: There's a guy who's way more successful than me at another studio. He thrives on chaos. I'd kill myself. If it's not running orderly, it just drives me nuts.

LARRY: In your showrunner experience was there a huge mistake you made?

ROBERT: I've made lots. The biggest was probably having Lois and Clark get married.

LARRY: Because that was the end of the tension. Classic.

ROBERT: All the warning signs were there. Everybody told me; my staff told me. I said, "I don't know how long we can keep this afloat. It just seems like a natural progression." And I was just so fucking wrong. I think I cost the show a year.

LARRY: How about the smartest thing you've ever done as a showrunner that you still draw on today?

ROBERT: When I gave up control of certain things—stopped micromanaging, started trusting people to do things—the shows ran better. The more you can do that, the more you can focus on the real problems as they arise.

LARRY: It's all about decision making, and delegating as much of that as possible.

ROBERT: I remember a guy doing his first show as executive producer asked, "What's the best advice you can give me?" I said, "Make decisions as they come up. If they're wrong, you can go back and correct 'em. But if they're sitting on your desk, you're going to get buried under the weight of them. If a guy comes to you and asks which gun to use for the scene, the Colt .45 or the Beretta, even if you don't know a goddamn thing about guns, pick a gun." Just keep making decisions. Some will be wrong; some will be great. But if it gets jammed up, you're not going to have time for the important stuff, which is to get the scripts right.

LARRY: You're known for coming onto a troubled show and righting the ship. Let's take *Hack*. Tell us how you fixed the situation there.

ROBERT: First, I told everybody to calm down. The problems in Philadelphia were not good, and I could not fix those as quickly as I fixed the *Lois and Clark* ones. That show was right there, on the Warner Brothers lot. So first I got the script thing righted, and that gave the staff here time to understand how things would work now. It just started being more orderly, and everybody took a big sigh of relief. As the season went on, I kind of got a better handle on how to make the show better. But that did not happen overnight. It was an evolution. The next year, I thought the scripts were, by and large, really good. I brought in a production designer I'd worked with before, and different location people. Immediately, the show looked better. So it's being able to identify those things, address the problem with good people, and get moving again.

LARRY: Sounds easier than it probably was.

ROBERT: *Hack* was really hard, because the show did not have the easiest concept. But we had these two really great actors in James Morse and Andre Braugher. I became very emotionally attached to the show, so it was tough for me when it got canceled.

LARRY: Michael, we've heard Bob's way of working with writers. What happens if you get a script that was done as promised in the outline, but somehow just doesn't work, and you're headed for preproduction?

MICHAEL CHERNUCHIN: If we had more time before prep, I'd give them every chance to try something else. Hopefully, whether the script works or not, something they did may spark something in me, and I may decide to take it another way. It's no reflection on their talent. I just got a different idea. Perhaps they created a great character, and it inspired me, and I decide to make the whole episode about that character. So I have to take it away and get it done before prep. People hate me for that, by the way, and it's important to know that it isn't about ego.

LARRY: It's just that it's your job to put the best show on the air.

MICHAEL: Yes.

LARRY: And what of that original idea, that original script—is it still potentially usable?

MICHAEL: Probably not. It's the same story, but told a different way.

LARRY: Is there a danger in these cases to harm writer morale?

MICHAEL: Yes, unfortunately, it can.

LARRY: But is it expected that the writer is a pro, so they need to deal with it?

MICHAEL: If you're in the major leagues, you must know how to turn a double play. I don't have the time to hold somebody's hand.

LARRY: But don't you have to somehow service staff morale? Even the greatest, most secure writer in the world is going to question his work if he's being totally rewritten.

MICHAEL: The smart writer has to ask why that was done and learn from it. I used to feel responsible for morale, but it just became "I must get through this." My job is too demanding.

LARRY: Why does a showrunner fail?

MICHAEL: You need a vision. You must be a leader, and people must respect you. Showrunners who are trying to keep everyone happy—they can't do that. You must have your blinders on and stick to your vision.

LARRY: What's one example of your vision on *Law & Order*?

MICHAEL: We used to say the perfect episode had six different characters expressing six different opinions about something, and they're all right. That's what you have to strive for. You can't just do a whodunit or try and get a political agenda across.

LARRY: So you have this obligation to the network because they have hired you. On the other hand, you have a vision. Where is the line between telling them, "You bought the show. This is my vision. Let me do it," and giving in to their demands because it's their money?

MICHAEL: I wish I knew. I was screaming on *Bull* [TNT]. I was a maniac. The notes from the network were, "They must be the best investment bankers on Wall Street." I said, "Okay." Then they said, "But they can't make any money," because they thought that making money was somehow bad! It's some bizarre rule of thumb. But what nobody understood, no matter how many times I told them, was that this *was not* a show about Wall Street. It was about *America. That America's business is business.* We got to a point where it was, "Change this or you're fired."

LARRY: Did you?

MICHAEL: Yes. Because sometimes you have to compromise.

LARRY: The nature of the business is compromise, isn't it?

MICHAEL: Why do you think there are women on *Law & Order*? We were told after the first year to put women on the show or we were fired.

LARRY: Because?

MICHAEL: Because they thought that's why the ratings were bad: there were no women. But see, there are many times they just misinterpret data that they have. Here's an example. I think there's a great opportunity for a show about the Supreme Court. But there were two recently that came out at the same time, and they both failed. Now there will never be, in my lifetime, another show about the Supreme Court. And their analysis is that "it's not interesting to the general public." And my analysis is, "No, the shows were bad."

LARRY: So how do you as a creator of a show, and as a writer, compromise between making something where nothing was before and serving commerce?

MICHAEL: Get an actor who's so big that the network can't say no.

LARRY: You must work within the system. It's the only way.

MICHAEL: Sure. Because executives have an agenda. They look to the past and see what works and do it again. They don't want to lose their jobs. Taking a chance on a crackpot like me, on this bizarre idea, they put themselves in jeopardy.

LARRY: Much easier to keep doing spin-offs of hit shows.

MICHAEL: And yet the best year in the history of TV was the first year of *NYPD Blue*. You never heard an executive say, "Get me another one of those!"

LARRY: Do you feel at all hamstrung by the way the business is run?

MICHAEL: Totally. The business is the thing now. Universal became NBC, which means I have to sell to NBC. Does NBC need an hour drama? And they'll order another *Law & Order* spin-off over anything new because they won't lose their job that way.

LARRY: What's your position about putting your name on a script? All showrunners rewrite.

MICHAEL: I don't put my name on scripts I rewrite. I'm the executive producer; I get all the credit anyway. I'm sure when I retire I'll see all those episodes without my name and regret all the residuals I gave up, but who cares?

LARRY: Who is your perfect staff writer?

MICHAEL: All I look for is smart people.

LARRY: What about writing?

MICHAEL: It's the ideas that are important. I want to see something I haven't seen before. I can fix dialogue. I can fix structure. Offer me something new. That's one of my big frustrations—jaded TV writers.

LARRY: Does that mean you'd read a sci-fi spec? Does that matter to you?

MICHAEL: I don't get it. It's not me. But I wouldn't turn it down. If something's interesting on the first page, I'll keep going.

LARRY: Would you be uncomfortable having five lower-level people without the experience of a number two?

MICHAEL: As long as they have good ideas.

LARRY: And what about how they work?

MICHAEL: I don't care. Come to the office. Live in Hawaii. I don't care. I have to be in the office because people are calling me all day. For most people coming to the office is a way to get away from their spouse. [Laughs]

LARRY: When I write, I do a draft specifically for actors. Hopefully, the story that exists is already so tight that every character has a clear objective. But I always do a special pass to make certain actors have a superobjective, or a goal. How about you?

MICHAEL: Not a special pass, but every scene I write I play it in my head. And if you do it right, you can cut half a scene that way, because it's what people don't say that's the most important. Nobody ever says what they really mean, and I was blessed with great actors who could convey that.

LARRY: Where is the intersection between an actor's voice and yours, the writer's? Do you give life to the character's voice, do the actors do it, or is it a cycle of endless building and supplementation?

MICHAEL: All of the above. I learned with Michael Moriarty that he said, "Sir." It flowed naturally. It rang, felt right for him, whereas other things feel right for Sam Waterston.

LARRY: Learning to write for an actor is just another way of elevating the material, isn't it?

MICHAEL: Yes, and that's why when I ran the show, we did table reads for every episode. You get the actors' input, you hear how they sound, we talk it through, explain the technical stuff so they can act it. Other showrunners tell me, "What are you talking to actors for? They got questions? I have an office."

LARRY: What about ego? That forestalls the creative process.

MICHAEL: Absolutely.

LARRY: And in an ideal world, there is no ego. But this is Hollywood, so it's there in everybody to some extent—

MICHAEL: Human nature.

LARRY: So, what happens when an actor crosses the line, when his ego gets in the way?

MICHAEL: I tell them. And the best actors know the difference between ego and the work, making the work better. Take Sam Waterston. Smart guy. Yalie. You know the old saying, "You can always tell a Yalie, but you can't tell them much." That's Sam. He always said he knows when he's lost the argument because I stare off into space and just start nodding. But I listen. He knows I do. But the final decision has to be mine.

LARRY: Why do actors become "problematic"? In my experience, it's the material they are uncomfortable with; they are insecure about it, or about themselves. And with good reason, because they're putting themselves out there. How do you deal with that?

MICHAEL: Make them part of the process. We have read-throughs, and they see that the notes they give actually do change the show. It doesn't work when showrunners don't treat the actors as partners and don't listen. Look, ultimately I get all the credit anyway, so why not listen? They play the character; they know them better than anyone. Why not listen?

LARRY: How do you handle your staff?

NEAL BAER: Get the structure down. Get the story down. When we're on the fourth or fifth pass, find people's attitudes and the message.

LARRY: Do you start with concept first, or message?

NEAL: Depends. I tell the writers, "Read, read, read." We have a full-time researcher. She'll pull articles galore. She'll talk to experts around the country. I tell writers, "Try to find the social kernel issue, but also the kernel of doubt." Like we have one about designer babies. To get to it is a twisting, turning, crazy show, but it does pose the question about whether we should choose the sex of our babies.

LARRY: What must a showrunner do to make a good show?

NEAL: I think many shows aren't serious about being very good. The most important thing I learned from John Wells is to make it as good as you can. John Wells is the best TV producer in Hollywood because he doesn't settle for mediocrity. He gets the best editors, composers, set designers, and the best directors.

LARRY: Isn't there a little thing called "budget" that gets in the way?

NEAL: It can when one's doing a show where budget is important. But budget was not important on *ER*, at least in the first seven years. It's just important to make it as good as it can be and not just settle. We never settle.

LARRY: I notice that many shows have director/producers.

NEAL: Actors love directors/producers. They sometimes trust them more than writer/producers because that's who's on the set with them. They have to deal with them emotionally in ways that a writer/producer can't.

LARRY: Some shows really give their writers responsibility, and some don't. Some want their writers writing; others want them more involved. How about you?

NEAL: You have to train writers to produce, because if they know how to produce, you'll make a better show.

LARRY: And it's right down to the supposed "little thing," isn't it? Like set design.

NEAL: Critical. One thing I learned on *ER* was kind of by accident. They were so lucky. They got a defunct hospital for a set, and added onto it: made the hallways wider and so on. You have great eye-line. You can see across the whole room. You can see through windows. But on this one pilot, I'll never forget—beautiful waiting room in Beverly Hills, narrow hallways, little sets. First time I watched this I said, "This show is dead because you cannot tell a story on this set." And guess what? Not long after, they were flying out in helicopters to playgrounds for stories where kids got shot. Then it became a show that did not know what it was because they did not know how to use the set, and the set is so critical to storytelling!

LARRY: It really is all integrated, isn't it? I remember Bob Zemeckis teaching at film school, and he said, "Everything must serve the story." He really meant *everything.*

NEAL: Exactly. So when I came on *Law & Order: SVU,* the first thing I ordered was to widen the hallways so that we can have more walk and talk, and build two interrogation rooms so that we can see into both at the same time. So it's always about the storytelling, and I think that that's just not understood often if you're going to manage/produce it.

LARRY: Vanessa, with *Jack and Bobby,* which you created, you were in a managerial position as well. What have you learned?

VANESSA TAYLOR: I've learned much about why rewriting is so difficult and why people don't preserve your work. Priorities are so different. I remember starting out and feeling like so-and-so took my script away, and that was mean, and why didn't they give me a chance? Now, I realize that the showrunner job is so difficult, so demanding on your personal life, that it becomes triage, where I'll be as sensitive as I can, but I'm going to do what's fastest. Otherwise, I'm not going to have any light at all. And nobody ever understands why I'm doing that, but at some point you've got to save yourself.

LARRY: Not sure that even the majority of staff writers understand that.

VANESSA: I don't think so. Who can? You feel like you've been hired, as you have, because of your writing, and you want to achieve the best. Sometimes that is not clear to people.

LARRY: You have hired people because they are great writers, and presumably because their writings have a voice that speaks to you. Now, you want to encourage them to use those talents, but at the same time, they need to be redirected to fit the vision of the show.

VANESSA: I also think there's a push-and-pull element to it. Greg Berlanti is very smart this way, very cognizant of the fact that one guy can't write a show. So you need to find the ways in which other people's voices can expand the potential of the show so that eventually they do fit on their own. In the beginning, you are steering them, to try to get the general gist, but as the show goes on, you can expand into different areas. I think he realized that an episode I wrote is going to sound very different from one that other writers do, and that was okay.

LARRY: Greg sounds like he understands what is needed to get the most from people.

VANESSA: Greg and I discovered very early on that I need a personal life. I really can't do it 24/7. I write fast, but I can't write till 4:00 a.m. If I can't have any weekends off, I just fall apart. And he realized this. It has made me more productive.

LARRY: Bryan, tell us your experience in rewriting yet also keeping the staff inspired.

BRYAN FULLER: Most of my time on *Wonderfalls* was spent rewriting and polishing. I never put my name on anybody's script because that's my job.

LARRY: That goes back to writer morale and what Bob said. If they know they're going to have their credit jumped, it really harms morale no matter how secure a writer is.

BRYAN: I don't really understand showrunners who behave that way. They're just shooting themselves in the foot. Regardless of how much you feel someone has contributed to a script, you can't start quantifying those things. The fact is that somebody is working their ass off and contributing, and if you start putting your name on things, it's just shitty and selfish. Your job as an executive producer is to homogenize the voice of the show that's coming in from all these different scripts.

LARRY: And sometimes that's a page 1 rewrite; sometimes it's a polish.

BRYAN: On first-year shows it's going to be much rewriting, because there's a huge learning curve. Many people think that staff writers either have it or don't, and that's a crock. They learn it if they don't have it. There's a great capacity for writers to learn. I think many people get egotistical, where it's "I have to do everything." It's a team, so you have to rely on them as a team. And I think the *Wonderfalls* staff worked best when we were rallying together to get a script out.

LARRY: Did it take you a while to find the voice for *Wonderfalls*?

BRYAN: Absolutely! That's why I don't believe in writing bibles for a show. Once you start moving in a direction, it can't be set in stone. It's set in wood.

LARRY: Because there are so many disparate elements that make up a show that you must be flexible.

BRYAN: It changes with every person that comes into contact with it, whether it is a writer or an actor. Everybody brings in different value. One actor on my show informed where that character is going by his personality and his acting style and his charisma. It was considerably different than the person we had originally cast in the pilot that he replaced. So the character became something a little bit different and significantly more interesting in my mind. It's the same with writers. We had so many writers who pitched ideas that took us in different directions and often weren't given the credit that they deserve because they're in The Room, doing their job, pumping out ideas.

LARRY: Are you saying that you're open to anything and make it work?

BRYAN: Not quite. Some ideas clearly don't work in the context of the show. Early on I gave notes on a script. I said, "A character just wouldn't do this." And one of the writers said, "They only have four lines in the pilot, so I don't know what they would do." A smart showrunner understands that. It's all developing, and much of it is still in my head that hasn't been articulated yet.

LARRY: So your job as showrunner is to assist that writer's creative process by articulating what's in your mind, but at the same time be open if somebody comes up with something that you hadn't thought of.

BRYAN: Absolutely, and frequently I'm wrong in those situations because I'll react negatively to something when they pitch it. After digesting it, I'll see what they were going for and go back to it, maybe even a week later. And sometimes an idea bites, and you're not quite sure what to do with it.

LARRY: It may be the wrong place at the wrong time. It's a matter of trusting your gut, as far as your vision of the show.

BRYAN: Yes, and also being open to your gut not always being right.

LARRY: Where did you pick all this up?

BRYAN: *Star Trek* in particular. I also learned much from *Wonderfalls*. At the start of this year, I was learning how to give notes on a script that's so different than what I expected. We're creative people, and sometimes it's hard to articulate the mess that's in our head. It's one thing to know if something doesn't feel right, but another to tell the writer *why*. That's something that you have to learn.

LARRY: The single biggest obstacle I've found is the inability of a show-runner to articulate his vision. Because if he can't, then the eager writer can't do his job, and then the showrunner just throws up his hands and does it himself, which is then demoralizing for the writer. How do you reconcile that?

BRYAN: It is very hard. We're under a tremendous amount of pressure, and things often have to be fixed immediately. I'm not perfect in any way, shape, or form, so I've made those mistakes with writers and have been abrupt in writing sessions, and then went down the hall afterwards and apologized. Thank God I realized it and was aware of it. I don't want to be the ass. That's not what I aspire to in my life.

LARRY: Because both a show and creativity are themselves organic and constantly in flux, even when you do articulate a vision, that doesn't mean it won't change.

BRYAN: It speaks to inherent flaws and the way television production is set up. Writing needs to start significantly earlier than production. Right now we have a two-month lead time, and that's just simply not enough. It's going to be beneficial to everybody if you have a four- to six-month lead time and you can get all these scripts done. It's easier all around, but the system just isn't set up that way.

LARRY: Because once the show gets the pickup, they want it on-air as soon as possible.

BRYAN: And the studio would have to pay the writers for four to six months, which they don't want to do. So it sets up these ridiculous expectations that drive everybody crazy.

LARRY: Now we have Aaron and Gretchen. Tell us your thoughts on what makes for a successful showrunner and a poor one.

GRETCHEN BERG: Like Laurie, what I liked so much about our showrunner on *Beverly Hills, 90210* is he had an agenda every day. Everybody felt like they were participating. Staffs fall apart if you are made to feel useless.

AARON HARBERTS: A weak showrunner is afraid of The Room, because that's the hardest part. It's fun to go to casting, to pick wardrobe, and have the prop guy show you this cool gun that he made. Poor show-runners avoid The Room, and then they don't use what's given to them from those sessions. When they finally do appear, they haven't seen the three hundred hurdles you've already jumped, so if they don't like a pitch, they think you've been lazy all day.

LARRY: Everything you're describing seems like it should be common sense. Why would they have a problem with this?

GRETCHEN: They weren't raised in television.

AARON: Or, as Bob just said, they're giving chances to people to run shows who don't have the experience.

GRETCHEN: So this is their one shot, using a bunch of strangers that they've hired because they had a good twenty-minute meeting.

AARON: The most effective are the ones who trust their staff. Our lower-level experiences were fabulous because even though the showrunners rewrote us, they trusted us to turn in a draft or break a story. Ineffective showrunners automatically think they've got to rewrite the entire first draft of a script because it has a few things wrong. Instead of putting writers through their paces, forcing them to learn the showrunner's voice—

LARRY: They think it's easier to just do it themselves.

AARON: Exactly. And then the showrunner perceives that they are the only one doing anything—

LARRY: Resenting everyone, 'cause they're allegedly not doing their "work."

AARON: It may take two scripts, but a good writer will learn how to write that show.

LARRY: Plus, if you just give someone one shot and fire them, then you're back at square one with another newbie.

GRETCHEN: We once had a showrunner talking about a staff writer, and he was really frustrated with him. I said, "I don't think he's even been given a chance." The showrunner said, "I'm not here to teach; that's not my job." And I thought, "But it *is* your job. Not to teach them *craft*, but to articulate your vision to them, and if you're a baby writer on your first job and not given the opportunity, then what's the point?"

LARRY: Hart, how do you handle rewriting your staff?

HART HANSON: I let writers know when I hire them that I will rewrite them if I want to, and I don't have to give a reason. They have to pretend they're okay with that. They can tell other writers that they're mad, but they can't tell me, and I don't want to see it in their eyes. It needs to be on my terms. I'm really sorry if I wreck something they've done, but the truth is they won't suffer from the series doing badly, but I will. However, when I am about to do my pass, I do ask, "Tell me about this story."

LARRY: Why do you think some showrunners tank?

HART: You must get a script to the director the first day of prep. If you don't, you're screwing everybody, unless you're a David Milch. I hate to say it, but a slightly less wonderful script is going to be a better show than a great script delivered late. I have a rule: you can complain about something up to twenty-four hours before a shoot. You can't come to me during blocking and say, "We have a huge hole, and somebody did not do their work."

LARRY: Neal, do you notice any common backgrounds among drama writers?

NEAL: Drama writers tend to be older. I haven't really worked with writers in their twenties who are really able to do it. Good drama requires understanding people, and that takes experience and maturity. I found this in medical school, too. I went as an older medical student, and I had an easier time than students who were twenty-two. We don't find it difficult to do the rectal exam because I've already got a kid.

LARRY: Are the writers who are really good with stories—are they coming from specific areas?

NEAL: On *Law & Order: SVU* we have a couple of journalists. One was an actor, and one was a psychologist in SVU. One writer came out of academia.

LARRY: Do you do much research for your show?

NEAL: Yes, we have these research books that are five to six hundred pages in length, and there are eight of them. On *ER* we just had phenomenal amounts of research done. We would talk to doctors, medical students, and nurses. We'd have guests for nurses' nights, ambulance nights, and get stories, stories, stories. We'd send the new writers to a real ER and a hospital, and make them spend a week there. Really get them into it, because I thought that was so critical, and you have to love it. I've worked with writers who don't have the passion for it, and it's very tough.

LARRY: I want to talk about the effect that *ER* had on television because it is demonstrative of good showrunning, and how it can affect story-telling as a whole.

NEAL: *ER* and *L.A. Law* had a huge impact on TV. They were the first shows to have real lawyers or doctors on the writing staff. It raised the bar for shows like *CSI* in that they all have experts on their writing staff because the audience has come to expect that.

LARRY: And yet, *Grey's Anatomy* doesn't seem to fit that mold.

NEAL: The medicine on *Grey's Anatomy* is completely wrong, but it doesn't matter because it's really not a medical show. It may have the same audience as *ER*, but I don't think they come with the same expecta-tions. Some people said, "*Grey's Anatomy* is *ER* for young people." I don't think that's true. *ER* was very popular amongst young people because they liked Sherri and George, and the struggle Noah had at age twenty-two, being the new kid on the block. Everybody could relate to that. *ER* was a very special kind of show that was popcorn but intelligent, so it could appeal on different levels for people with different story appetites. *Grey's Anatomy* has those archetypal ele-ments in the characters, but the medicine is secondary to the soap.

LARRY: In my memory, all the shows about medical students save *ER* have failed. Why is *Grey's Anatomy* working?

NEAL: It's a soap slotted directly after *Desperate Housewives*, which has a huge lead-in. Lead-ins are so important. The show takes a *Desperate Housewives* audience and gives them sex in the hospital.

LARRY: *ER* was almost always about life and death.

NEAL: Yes, which gave it an immediacy that's not there in many shows. So it was not just pressing the gurney at the door, but it was asking how are the doctors going to deal with these horrible medical dilem-mas. Every episode had some kind of medical dilemma that was not black-and-white, and you would see what the doctors were made of by their decision. George Clooney's character would be willing to take the hospital down if it meant finding out which pills were placebos and which were real to get a kid out of pain. He was an interesting character; you understood him. You also understood that he had many foibles, but was passionate about saving kids' lives. Or the Gloria Reuben story, where *ER* was the first show to put a character on who was HIV positive, who lived a life that was not one of suffering but of helping others. That was unheard of. And as medicine changed, so did the show. So it did things that hadn't been seen before too but always accurately, because we knew that the public got their medical information from television.

LARRY: Carol, what's changed for you in terms of writing, now that you are a showrunner?

CAROL BARBEE: I've gotten faster. I had to. Every deadline is my deadline. I trust myself more. I worry less about whether every word I write is great. And the lack of fear, I really believe, has made me a much better writer.

LARRY: There aren't many female showrunners these days, and I'm wondering if you can articulate any gender differences that exist in either your management or creative processes.

CAROL: I'm not sure I can characterize any gender differences there. That's a great question. I certainly pattern my management style after Bob DeLaurentiis's. I suppose my "mom energy" does influence how I deal with people, how I handle and respect them. I want them to be happy creatively but also make sure they understand their job. I try to think about why someone might be acting out if they're unhappy.

LARRY: Finally, Carol, I'm really interested in trying to understand each writer's own personal writing mandate. Do you think you've developed one?

CAROL: I try to write with an open heart. I try to write what I think is true. I feel a responsibility about what I put into the world. That responsibility extends to the people I work with as well as the audience.

LARRY: Jason, we've talked a bit about finding great writers, but allowing them to use their talents and voice, but also needing to fulfill your vision of a show. What's your approach when you're running a show?

JASON KATIMS: I've gone through an evolution as a showrunner from being less inclusive to being more so. I realized television is a vicious medium because it's relentless. There are so many stories to tell, so many things to figure out, so little time to do it, and at some point you've got to look at these brilliant writers and let them into the process. People will gravitate to certain characters. By giving them a stake in it, you make your show better. If you can do that in a way where the show is being improved, and you have a trustworthy staff, you have a better show.

LARRY: You seem somewhat unique in that you really allow your writers' individual voices to come out, yet still do a pass to bring the show into a sphere where the audience still recognizes it as the show. Does a writer need to be adaptive to your voice to be successful?

JASON: There needs to be a basic affinity for the characters. Whether the writer can write the show has to do with things that are not easy to ascertain. I was able to write *My So-Called Life* pretty well because I had an affinity with every single one of those characters.

LARRY: Ultimately, there's no real way to discern if a writer can do that or not.

JASON: The only thing that I've noticed is that if you listen to people when they come in and interview, in five minutes they'll tell you everything. They'll tell you what their motivations are for being on the show, how hard they really want to work on the show, that they really don't like the show or if they love it, or if they truly believe that they're the person to do it. I think that's a really important part of it. One of the most important things with writers is who they are as people, and how they work. Also, I've learned what I need.

LARRY: Which is what?

JASON: Aggressive people to do storytelling, to pitch ideas, develop ideas from other writers that are being pitched, be tenacious, and break a story fast.

LARRY: The more mechanical aspects of the process?

JASON: Well, that's not mechanical.

LARRY: Isn't it? There's an element of problem solving in terms of structure.

JASON: To me, the breaking-story thing is about getting the group of people that you assembled to work as a team, work well together, and not feel like there's backstabbing. What happens is you're in The Room and you're breaking story, and, yeah, it's mechanical, but what you want is them to not only be open but to be dying to bring their souls to it. It's an amazing idea, what happens in a story room. It's at the heart of this combination between business and art. Here you are, saying, "Okay, we've got to come up with this story, but at the same time bring emotion to it, fast."

LARRY: It really is unique. Every show I've ever been on, there's been camaraderie among the writers. We do get to know each other pretty well, and The Room can often turn into a confessional. All sorts of odd things come out—one woman told me she once smoked crack with Ted Kennedy—but these are real stories that give scripts that emotion you need.

JASON: I took over *Boston Public* in its third year. It just ran itself. You delivered a script; they would shoot it.

LARRY: The problems crop up when people interfere with the vision.

JASON: Too many cooks, whether it's within production, at the studio, or network, can kill you. It breaks down the system. I've often said that's what writers get their paycheck for. We're not getting paid because we're writing, because that we would do for free. We're getting paid to, in a mature and constructive way, deal with all the obstacles to us doing a show. It could be you're going in one direction and you're dealing with all the executives, and then the president of the network finally gets around to watching an episode, and suddenly you're hit with a barrage of contradictory notes.

LARRY: And if everybody's not on the same page, there's not enough communication.

JASON: There's never enough communication, but how could there be? Think about what they're doing. A studio and its network have all of these shows. The presidents are dealing with corporate issues, and then there's development department execs versus current, there's God knows other corporate issues, so that's when it can be a real challenge. That's the toughest part of writing for television.

LARRY: You really have to be on the same page with your studio and your network.

JASON: What makes it difficult is that the process gets screwed up, and it slows the process down, and the process *can't slow down*. When showrunners get testy, as we all have, it's really because of that. I believe you can always agree creatively. The truth is it's show *business*; it's not show *art*. Writers and actors—we all chose to do it; nobody put a gun to our head and said, "Go write for television." Part of it is that the networks need people to watch the shows, and they're sometimes going to have more educated opinions than we have about that audience. Where it gets hairy is when the outlines are approved and you give them the script, and suddenly you're getting notes that don't jibe with what you've heard before. Somewhere there's been a change. People are human. That happens. You learn as you go, and they're learning as they go, too.

LARRY: Well, this is the real collision of art and commerce. I think you're right, that reasonable people can disagree creatively, and hopefully on that basis alone, the showrunner is given the benefit of the doubt. But these are corporate entities, and it isn't really about entertainment. It's about making money so they can survive as a business concern, and that means getting the audience to watch. The problem comes when corporate believes that by interfering creatively that it will increase the number of viewers. Now sometimes they may be right, but I think we all know when we're watching good television and when we're watching bad television.

JASON: You have to be able to know when the network has a note that's right. You've got to know when you're not right, or that the best thing right now is to change it because—

LARRY: It's not worth fighting about.

JASON: Yes, and you're right. The biggest thing is not what they say, and not the fact that they have opinions; it's when those things get in the way of the showrunner's movement. I remember early on having a long phone conversation with the network about some note, and on and on and on we went. Then another studio person on the call rang me back and said, "Jason, you don't have to do all this. We're just listing the notes. Say 'Thanks,' and if you address half of the notes, they'll be thrilled."

LARRY: A major part of this collision is that there is no way to predict what will succeed. From uncertainty comes fear. That's how it also works in the stock market. And when you are afraid, you either run away or try to control or fix something. So a network or studio will, understandably, want to try and insert itself more into the process. So, on a showrunner level, they sense the fear, and their confidence gets undermined. If you're a first-timer, you've got much on the line, and you want to please them, so there's this tendency to just throw entire scripts out. Tim, have you seen this happen?

TIM KRING: I don't have the nerve for that. Many people like being on the edge, and they like maintaining control. Part of the controlling process is to always have it slightly out of control. I have too much anxiety and lose too much sleep over things. I'd much rather do the hard work and stick to something.

LARRY: So what's your managerial approach to writing?

TIM: I let people find their own process. I hired them because they were writers. They obviously figured something out on their own before they got onto my show. I need to be let in on that process and give a seal of approval so I don't get big surprises. We keep those to a minimum because every story gets a tremendous amount of Room time. Hence, the need for outlines. You see things in an outline to catch problems.

LARRY: Do you feel like you're able to let your writers' voices come out?

TIM: I do, and I think it's done out of necessity. But there's a benefit of having other writers' voices on the show, especially during the first season, when we were trying to figure out what the show is. I never had the luxury of being confident of what it was that I wanted to do. I'm always looking at somebody else's writing and saying, "Is that more of what I should be?" There's always that questioning going on in my mind.

LARRY: That's a very Zen thing. Letting go of your singular vision and letting the staff help you find it.

TIM: I really try to embrace other writers showing me what the show can be. When it worked I had that great epiphany of "Oh, we could do this also." I had no idea the show could absorb a certain tone, and I did not know the boundary of the show was actually as far as it has been. You fall off a cliff a few times by going too far, but at least you learn where the boundary is.

LARRY: And you're not afraid to take it there. I was always the guy in start-up shows saying, "Let's play this episode backwards."

TIM: I totally relate to that. We've been wildly eclectic on *Crossing Jordan*, and I'd like to say that it's all by design. I think that some lack of vision has led to some happy accidents. Of everything I've said, this is probably the most important thing: there's an organic quality to making a TV show, and if you hold too tightly to an idea of what you think a show is going to be, you're going to end up strangling the show. The show needs to tell you what it wants to be, and characters need to tell you who they want to be. Every character on this show started out as a different person. I could have never in my wildest dreams imagined where some of these characters went. So much of that is the actor giving voice to things that you never realized.

LARRY: I always thought of it as an organism. Everything has to work in tandem for the organism to grow and let it breathe.

TIM: You have to, because how can you compete for new viewers or hold on to regular viewers if you're not evolving the show? I think the reason where shows fail is egos get in the way. The showrunner feels the need to push his own voice.

LARRY: And we're back to not demoralizing your staff.

TIM: Right, and being a motivational manager is a big part of the job. Motivate and empower. I learned much being in situations where I was not empowered. When we started this show, me and Alan [Arkush] and Dennis [Hammer] had discussions about the kind of environment we wanted. We'd all worked for bullies, and had situations that were interpersonally unpleasant. We decided early on that we were going to be a place that empowered people. I think we've for the most part held to it.

LARRY: Is it possible to overdelegate, overempower?

TIM: Everybody produces their own episodes and are involved from day one with every aspect of production, and given a tremendous of authority. The upside is when it succeeds, it succeeds hugely, and you've turned a story editor into a bona fide producer. How do you ever envision a life of going home to your kids if you're not creating a system where people can actually do some of the work that you do? But when it doesn't work, people can drown.

LARRY: Who drowns and who doesn't?

TIM: The drowners are those who could not connect interpersonally, who held on too closely to things and were not flexible. Being flexible is everything. It's a marathon and not a sprint. There are twenty-two episodes to do, and the production needs dictate what you can and can't do. We often have situations where you write a scene, go to the production meeting, and get told, "We loved this scene in the convention center with three hundred extras, beautifully written and fabulous. What we have is a Volkswagen, and it's got a backseat." If you can't say, "I love the Volkswagen," then you're in trouble.

LARRY: Which is probably where film school came in handy for both of us because we were so restricted. We know how to embrace the Volkswagen.

TIM: That's the amazing thing. So often when you hold on, the vision is not completely fulfilled, yet the product of one plus one sometimes is three. You get a much more intimate scene. People cried, and I wouldn't have gotten that in the convention center. You have to take the long view on these things.

LARRY: Ego and insecurity run contrary to television, it seems.

TIM: The accolades of having a show on the air are plenty, and there's plenty to go around. Because I created the show, I've discovered what everybody else discovered: I always get the blame and the credit no matter what I did anyway. By bringing out the best in people, I think I have lots of people who go to bat for me.

LARRY: With the sensitivity you've developed towards the staff, is giving notes a challenge?

TIM: I can give notes with a friend, which is how I regard my writers. The bad part is when they really don't get it right and you have to rewrite them, and you're diminishing their sense of themselves.

LARRY: But given the environment you created, where the writer knows they are valued, perhaps that blow doesn't hurt as much.

TIM: You're right. We do soften the blow by creating an environment where everybody's able to get over their own failures.

LARRY: To what extent do you share show politics with the staff?

TIM: We've had a very difficult road, and I chose not to keep it private. I aired all my anxiety about it.

LARRY: I would appreciate that as a writer.

TIM: Maybe that's been a mistake at times, because I've created anxiety where it did not need to be, but I also felt that it humanized their connection to the show and to me. The reluctance of being a boss has been difficult in the having to think about the show as a whole and not somebody's personal needs. I could spend eight hours of my day writing thank-you notes, sending flowers, and calling people to say what a great job they did. I wish I had that kind of time. It's hugely important to tell somebody that they're doing a good job. You find that it pays such dividends to be someone who's gregarious in that way. It helps the whole process. A lesson that I learned in working with people, and it's a mistake that the studios and the network make all the time, is that anybody worth their salt is not doing it for the money. As soon as you realize that, it forces you to deal with them on a completely different level. They're really there because they love what they're doing; they want to do the best the can. So the empowerment and the encouragement become far more important to them than getting paid.

LARRY: How do you choose whom to hire?

TIM: When you read stuff and you're trying to hire people, it's impossible. You're reading some spec.

LARRY: So it's more about your vision of the utopian staff?

TIM: It becomes so much more about who they are and their energy and their enthusiasm. It's much more about putting together a dinner party than it is getting all these great writers together. I take enthusiasm and personality over talent. I'll carry somebody that I like.

LARRY: You really seem to prefer to feel your way through things.

TIM: I just don't overthink much, and people who want to do that constantly confront me. They want to do "Is this black or is it green? Why don't you know the answer to this?" I want to say, "I don't know the answer to it, and leave me alone!" But to add to what Bob Singer said, part of being a showrunner is you have to pretend you know the answers to things. You're constantly feeling like you're faking your way through it. I have no opinion about some things, and yet somebody needs me to have an opinion.

LARRY: You approach writing the same way?

TIM: Yes. I don't have a strong intellectual sense of where I want to go with it. I have a feeling that makes me tap into feelings of universality with your fellow man. I know that at the end I want to feel like the song that I heard on the radio—not the words of the song, just the way it made me feel. I have to be left alone to do that.

LARRY: Peter, what's your approach to showrunning?

PETER LENKOV: I don't believe in being a hard-ass to anybody. Everybody's a human being. Why be rude because you're in a position of "power"? You want everybody to feel they're part of the team and to give their best.

LARRY: Is it analogous to being a football coach?

PETER: More a quarterback than a coach. A quarterback goes in there as part of the team; a coach gets you to do your best, and that means sometimes screaming at people. Sometimes a coach hasn't even played ball. They're good with strategy, they're good with organization, they're good with motivation, but they're not on the field getting tackled.

LARRY: Still, though, some writers just don't work out.

PETER: Unfortunately. They may feel you're being hard on them because you have to let them go.

LARRY: Owing to the writing or their ability to work with other people?

PETER: Sometimes it's writing; sometimes it's whether they fit in The Room; sometimes they make themselves the odd man out. It goes back to what I said about being intimidated, so they're not contributing, which builds to a point where their utility is questioned. I think everybody's got a chance to score a touchdown. It's up to you as the individual what you do with the ball. Give me something—contribute to the show.

LARRY: Do you enjoy working with new writers?

PETER: Very much. On *The District*, our researcher pitched an idea for a character that we all loved. He'd never written a script, so as a co–executive producer, I took it upon myself to work with him on it. I saw this kid go from never having put a word down to coming up with a finished draft of a script. It was an amazing process. I really enjoyed it. And I'll always be proud of that time we spent together, because I feel like I made a difference in where he's going to go with his career.

LARRY: We should talk more about that mentor relationship. I had one in Jeff Melvoin.

PETER: Most people wouldn't be here without somebody like that in their lives.

LARRY: Who was that for you?

PETER: Joel Surnow.

LARRY: How did Pam Veasay run *The District*?

PETER: She ran it incredibly tight but was a big believer in having a life. You know, just the fact that we did ten thirty to six or seven at night demonstrated her respect that people have other things to do. She was a big believer in putting a board up, breaking down every act by scene. She was big on using colored marker to show what each character's arc was. I preferred that, because I felt like I could walk into a room and know where the show is going.

LARRY: Shawn, let's get away from talking about staffs and get into *The Shield*. What's the most challenging thing about running that show?

SHAWN RYAN: It is a very difficult show to write—although I'm sure everybody thinks whatever show they're on is difficult to write—but it really is because we're cognizant of not doing anything that violates what we've done in the past. There has to be something that in the present is exciting to watch and feels real and yet leaves us possibilities to go someplace in the future.

LARRY: The show has the most realistic feeling of any cop show.

SHAWN: Audiences are very aware of how things are made now. One thing that always drove me crazy about TV was the music. Here were wonderfully written, acted, and directed shows, and this music would kick in, telling me how to think about this scene. It was so frustrating. I don't like feeling manipulated. *The Shield* was my backlash against some shows. I want people to feel like a fly on the wall. If we can't write a scene, act it, direct it, and edit it in a way that powerfully conveys what we want to get across, then that's the scene's problem. That's not a music problem. So we make the scene work, or I'll cut it.

LARRY: And this is all aided by your camera work as well.

SHAWN: Visuals are not my expertise.

LARRY: But from *Homicide: Life on the Street*—same thing: no score.

SHAWN: *Homicide* was a documentary attempt. *The Shield* I describe as observational. I'm always trying to hold us back a little. It's a natural instinct to want your talent to be noticed, and yet I do not want people to notice the writing, the directing, the acting, and I really don't want them to notice the camera work. It should all work in concert to make them notice *the show*.

LARRY: Many times I'll watch some show and say, "God, that's such a beautiful scene." I could never say that about your show.

SHAWN: We're the one show where you walk into the makeup trailer and come out looking worse.

LARRY: A show like yours gives you an opportunity to grind an ax, yet I haven't seen that.

SHAWN: I have opinions, and I try to sneak them into the show, but I never try to blur them.

LARRY: What's the demographic of your audience? Male or female?

SHAWN: In the past it's been 60 percent male, 40 percent female. This year those numbers got a little bit closer.

LARRY: So much of the show has elements that I think male audiences appeal to, on a thematic level. Loyalty, honor, team versus individual, family versus work.

SHAWN: We all have rules in our jobs and lives that we all instinctively understand, and we feel like they prevent us from behaving the way we want to behave. So here we give you Vic Mackey, whom you know may do bad things, but if your daughter's taken, he's going to do everything possible to get her back.

LARRY: Your show premiered right before 9/11. Do you think that had an effect on its success?

SHAWN: All of a sudden cops and firemen were heroes. It made our show five times more valuable than it was before, because we were asking the question on the micro level: "What are we allowing our law enforcement officers to do in order to keep us safe?" All of a sudden that question was so much more important.

LARRY: How do you handle reading people for hiring?

GARDNER STERN: We all read scripts, and we get sent a ton. Then, before you even read you'll hear something good about someone, so you pull that one out of the pile. I can read ten pages and can tell.

LARRY: Because either they can write or they can't.

GARDNER: I don't need to read a whole script unless I want to see how they formulate a story. So then, if they pass muster with one person, we bring them in. As I said before, much of what is going to get them a job here is personality. So you just want to meet them and talk to them.

LARRY: Based on where you are now, Gardner, do you feel any obligation towards studio or network suggestions on writers?

GARDNER: No. The network and studio have to sign off on upper-level hires, so to that extent you have to involve them, but I feel absolutely no obligation whatsoever to hire anybody they recommend.

LARRY: Do you consciously ignore anyone they recommend?

GARDNER: No, it's not like you need to be an asshole.

LARRY: Gardner, what's the key to hiring the right people?

GARDNER: Process and personality. There're eight of us, and we're together all the time. If the personalities don't mesh, it's not as pleasant.

KIM NEWTON: That sitcom-room thing applies to drama just as well, very much so.

LARRY: Gardner, you seem to have created a show where The Room is a safe place to be. Is that a management style you consciously developed?

GARDNER: Nope. Wish I had. I've always been fairly laid back. But it's true: you can't edit yourself, because all that stuff contributes to a better story.

KIM: I've worked on shows that had a very hierarchical Room where you did not speak if you were at a certain level. You could see people dying to contribute.

LARRY: Yeah, I was on a show where you'd say something, and you were just waiting for one of the showrunners to say the most insulting thing to see which one could top each other. Boy, was *that* productive.

GARDNER: It's interesting when you talked about having your dreams crushed, and you asked earlier, "Do you still consider the script yours after it's rewritten?" When you reach a certain level, particularly executive producer, one of the greatest rewards is you're finally in a position where no one can tell you to take your favorite line out. When you're dealing with the network or the studio, and they say, "Do we really need to say that?" you're in a position where you can say, "Yes." Now they're in the position of demanding you change something, which by extension implies that they know more about it than you do, which also then brings up the subject of why are they paying me all this money? You sort of trap them.

KIM: You have to pick those battles wisely.

GARDNER: I love those moments, and I think the networks and studios don't respect you unless you say that to them. I created one show that got on the air. They loved the pilot, so we did a second episode. Then they had all these notes that came out of nowhere. I told them if they did not like this episode, then we're talking about two different series. They eventually backed down. I went a little overboard in that case to make a point, but when you say, if their notes go to the heart of the series—

LARRY: And if they do, what then?

GARDNER: You must decide if it's something you really care about. Unless you care about it, it's going to be tough to come to work. So you must put your foot down and ultimately be willing to get fired. We've all heard stories about showrunners who fought with the studio and got fired, but that's a chance you've got to take. One can have a more cavalier attitude like that if you have a level of confidence in your ability to get hired again.

LARRY: Okay, as you go into your fourth season do you think you've earned the right to do something totally off the wall?

GARDNER: That's what this show is all about. And that's unusual. On most other dramas, if you started doing that stuff, it would be jumping the shark. Crazy shit can happen as long as it makes sense.

LARRY: Sounds like Hollywood. No, wait, crazy shit happens and *never* makes sense!

Chapter 9 Lesson

Most people want to be in charge. It doesn't matter what the business is. They want to be the director or CEO or engineer or prime minister or president. They figure that it gives them the freedom to do what they want, which is a good thing, because they know better than everyone else anyway. Whatever it is, they are sure it will run smoother and better if they are the bosses.

Put all that nonsense out of your mind. It'll kill you.

So why be a showrunner if you can't enjoy all that stuff?

It's still about process. You just have more of a hand in it. So now you had *really* better enjoy it!

Once you actually become a showrunner, the first thing you'll realize (although you'll know it, already having worked your way through the ranks) is that you need many people to help bring your show to life. Television is not an auteur's medium. You need writers, just like the kind you were not so long ago. You need to articulate your vision to them, so they can execute your creative desires. You have to trust them. You have to give them a chance to succeed and not fire them after their first script reads nothing like what you envisioned.

All CEOs and showrunners must remember that a company or a television show is a living, breathing organism. Although it may appear that its employees, its processes, and its products depend on individuals, this belief is only an illusion. As mentioned earlier, writers must be conscious of their contribution to the whole for the show to succeed.

As a showrunner, you have to honor the contributions of the people you have hired. What's the point of hiring a staff of writers if you are just going to completely rewrite them anyway? They are there to help, not to usurp. This attitude is why Jason Katims has such a strong reputation. He knows to let his writers reach The Zone and will only rewrite them as necessary.

A showrunner must delegate. You cannot do everything yourself. Find someone to supervise postproduction for you so you aren't locked in an editing room all day, isolated from your writers. Once again, delegating

requires trust. This point is true for every department head—from production design to cinematography to makeup. Still, you have to keep an
eye on them so they understand the vision of the entire show and execute
their own creativity in service of it.

Showrunning is, at its core, no different from any top position in any
organization. As much as you might hope that it involves exclusive focus
on the creative aspects of the show that you have created, the truth is that
you'll probably spend the least amount of time actually being creative.
Oh, you'll spend time writing—rewriting, actually—but all the heartache
you've endured to bring your vision to the small screen is going to get lost
amid the actual job of running a show. You might write the season opener
and maybe the finale, but forget about writing any original scripts during
the season.

You will have to rewrite other people's scripts. That process can be
painful for them and you, but you must guide the show as you see fit.
And, of course, you must try to do so from The Zone.

You'll have to deal with the studio and the network and possibly
even a separate production company—and you may have as many as
fourteen people giving you notes on *your* show. Somehow, you'll have
to understand the ever-shifting political landscape enough to pretend
that you are listening to them when they tell you stupid things, actually listen and respond when they say something great, tell them not to
interfere when they get nervous because ratings aren't what they hoped
for, but be flexible enough to admit that your vision isn't playing and
you'll need to alter it if you want to stay on the air. Meanwhile, you have
to make sure you don't bust the budget they've given you (which isn't
enough), and keep the other hundred production employees feeling like
they are valued.

Somewhere in here, you have to keep your ego in check so you don't
become a raving lunatic if your show is a hit. If you do go crazy, your writing staff will slowly grow to hate you, and, unless they fear not finding
another job, they'll find another job, and you won't have those people who
helped make the show a success around anymore.

It helps to be a raving lunatic, however, if your actors become prima
donnas and need to be reminded that they are not central to your show,

like *Law & Order*, and can be fired at will. On the other hand, if you've had those acting classes I've prodded you to take, you also value your actors tremendously because of the priceless things they can bring to their characters and the show. You can also speak their language and keep them creatively satisfied.

You have to listen to everyone's contributions, because one idea can change an entire series for the better, but if you listen to everyone all the time, you'll never make a decision and undermine your own vision—which will likely result in script delays and productions shutdowns and cost you the job.

You want to be both loved and occasionally feared, but not feared in such a way that your writers don't regard you as a friend when they want to discuss core creative struggles with someone they respect and admire.

On the other hand, if you are or choose to be a lunatic, that decision does not inhibit the possibility of success. Some showrunners are mentally disturbed, thrive on chaos, and ignore every single rule of how to run a smooth show, but have enjoyed such success in the past and present that nobody will challenge them because network television is in such a bad place that a network will do anything to keep a show with an 11 share on the air.

So you could, in theory, *pretend* to be a raving lunatic as long as audiences watch your show. This deception may, in fact, allow you by sheer force of will to keep your show on the air because you will scare the executives into never telling you no or saying, "You've been canceled."

So when you become a showrunner and figure it all out, give me a call. I want to know the secret. I want to know "why."

Further Reading

Bennis, Warren. 2009. *On Becoming a Leader.* New York: Basic Books.

Parcells, Bill. 1995. *Finding a Way to Win: The Principles of Leadership, Teamwork, and Motivation.* New York: Doubleday.

Useem, Michael. 1999. *The Leadership Moment: Nine True Stories of Triumph and Disaster and Their Lessons for Us All.* New York: Three Rivers Press.

10

Case Study: *Tim Kring and* Heroes

Tim Kring, the creator and showrunner of *Heroes,* pulls together all of the elements discussed. For some writers, creativity is born from a primordial soup, much like the one mankind emerged from. In Tim's case, creativity was prepared from scratch, its ingredients delicately simmered in a broth for years before serving. Those ingredients included a dreamy childhood ensconced in the counterculture of 1960s San Francisco, exercises in the visual arts, a blend of Judaic and Christian theological studies, and a love of cinematography.

The result is that Tim developed into a very soulful individual, with an almost uncanny ability to empathize with people of every stripe. Those individuals who watched *Crossing Jordan* or *Heroes* will likely notice those traits apply to the characters. Even the dead in *Crossing Jordan* were treated as if they were still living, such was the sensitivity shown to them.

At the same time, Tim has developed an expert sense of craft through his years as a television writer. But what he has subsequently achieved is that critical balance that successful television writers must have: an ability to straddle the worlds of emotion and craft. More important, he creates a work environment that allows his staff to do the same.

So what about Tim's creative process has made him a survivor in television? I believe it is the prism through which he and his characters view life and interact with others. It is not just Tim's ability to relate to or even empathize with a character in a situation that makes his characters intriguing. He has an ability to actually reach back and reconnect with specific felt emotions of a certain moment in his life, much in the way that actors utilize the emotional memory technique.

His shows also demonstrate a reverence for life, as well as presenting a sense of its fragility and its sacredness. There is also a spiritual center to his dramatic situations. In *Heroes* a group of disparate individuals from all over the world simultaneously experience physical changes that endow them with various abilities. However, instead of treading the familiar ground one might expect of a superhero-origin story, we are instead treated to each character's failings as they struggle to find their new place in the world.

Tim described this project as being his most personal to date. He referred to it as "the bastard child of *The Incredibles* and *Eternal Sunshine of the Spotless Mind*," two movies he saw in a twenty-four-hour period. The former film provides the genre for his characters to inhabit, although the latter provides a spiritual and emotional core to their plight. In this case, however, Tim has been afforded the luxury of an episodic venue for his exploration of characters within this genre. Whereas the recent filmic treatments of seminal comic book heroes have given us specific examinations of these characters, television gives us the opportunity to examine them in the way a graphic novel does—with infinitely more depth.

Thematically, the show allows Tim and his writers to explore very human themes: the struggle to find one's purpose in the world and the burden once that purpose is discovered, the necessity to *matter*, the feeling that we must leave behind something of value before we die. Fans of *Crossing Jordan* will recognize these themes, for the characters in the Boston medical examiner's office struggle with these issues themselves, and also feel an obligation to make certain that the people they encounter in death are not forgotten. For them, finding justice ensures they are not forgotten. So, too, for the characters of *Heroes*.

How does Tim achieve this success? First and foremost, he creates his work from the haven of The Zone. Second, he navigated the random set of events that befell him to emerge as a showrunner. So even though he was faced with those elements of the business that he could not control, he was prepared because he produced great work.

I caught up with Tim after the third season of *Heroes* to discuss how his creative process changed as a result of the show's success.

LARRY: So here we are four years after our first discussion. In the interim, you created *Heroes,* and it's become a global phenomenon. Let's talk about how your writing and creative processes changed with this project.

TIM KRING: It was a giant undertaking, this multicharacter storytelling. The characters were disconnected for the first ten episodes, so there were eight different storylines. It became apparent that the story engine would be different with a serialized drama than a closed-ended one.

LARRY: Eats up more story than you think?

TIM: Yes, and one becomes more efficient as a storyteller, and we play "Name That Tune," where a writer thinks they can do a story in six beats, but realizes they can do it in three. It becomes a kind of haiku storytelling. So what we thought would take twelve episodes instead takes five.

LARRY: That must change the dynamic in The Room.

TIM: This approach needs a tremendous amount of time to break story and many people to do it. We also had to do it quickly, because we got picked up in mid-May and had to be on air in mid-September.

LARRY: And this is what led to each writer being assigned to follow a character storyline through several episodes, rather each person writing an entire episode?

TIM: We had to take advantage of cross-boarding the show. If we told a story that took place in Claire's house over four episodes, it was better for the production to go to that location, drop anchor, and shoot all that footage right then. So we needed all those shows written and prepped. This meant every writer had to change what their traditional role might be on a regular show. Usually, you write your own episode, and you can't help but be protective of your own stuff. It's human nature. Here, we could not do that. Everybody had to chip in on every episode.

LARRY: I think you took a real risk. On shows that aren't run well, the feelings of competitiveness and jealously can really poison a staff.

TIM: That was eliminated under this process, although there was some grumbling at first. Some folks had a tough time letting go of their ego. We're writers. We need to shine. This is natural and very human, and we had very vocal conversations about it. Plus, it was a high-end staff, people of showrunner level, so they had an expectation about how much say they'll have in the show's direction, and how much their own voice will come through. But everyone sublimated their ego in deference to the work, because we had to rely on each other to get the work done—there was so much of it.

LARRY: I'm guessing that meant weeks breaking story, but then the scripts must've come together quickly.

TIM: We broke story for three weeks, and then a week or so later, we assembled four scripts. So in the span of five days, we went from nothing to two hundred pages of teleplay! And we all looked at each other, and said, "This just might work."

LARRY: What happened next?

TIM: Once assembled by the group, we talk about each script, and everybody polishes their storylines. We reassembled the scripts, and then handed each one off based on whoever was first in line. The person who got a script became the writer of record on that episode and was responsible for seeing it through.

LARRY: The danger of this process seems like it would lend itself to creating episodic, choppy shows.

TIM: Yes, so we spent much time talking transitions and interconnectiveness—which is the overall theme of the show. And once the writer of record gets it, it's his job to put all that connective tissue in.

LARRY: What other dividends did this process pay?

TIM: It created a staff cohesiveness like I had never seen. There was an attachment to the material where everyone felt committed to every script. Because we did not actually assign the script until late in the process, you had to be wholly committed to every story in The Room because you may be assigned to write it. The real benefit was, I felt, when you look at Season 1, there's an incredible consistency from show to show.

LARRY: Normally when breaking story by episode, you move around in nonlinear fashion. You could not have been able to do that.

TIM: Everything was predicated on a simple question: "What happens next?" So you do a scene and ask, "What happens next?"

LARRY: That's the way Glenn Caron worked. It was kind of a shock not to work nonlinearly. It does provide a kind of strict logic to every step.

TIM: We wrote in sprints of four episodes. We only saw that far ahead, and then a new set of problems would arise that our characters had to face. We had big signposts we wanted to get to, but always got to them faster than we expected. So we learned by iteration and mistakes, and it made for a dynamic process. And we learned that stuff did not work.

LARRY: Like what?

TIM: Storylines we thought would be great weren't, or we might get two people together and find they don't have chemistry. We might see dailies and realize that we've invested the rest of the season in these two characters that just weren't clicking on-screen. So we had to dump that whole storyline. Or perhaps we got an actor, but then he got a feature film offer, and we only got him for two episodes—so we had to kill him.

LARRY: And therein lies the collision between art and commerce, or art and the real world.

TIM: It's very organic, and viewers need to understand that the nature of series TV is that you are at the mercy of many variables, especially with serialized drama. If you lean too heavily on a plan, you're screwed!

LARRY: Let's talk more about serialization's pros and cons.

TIM: Serialized storytelling is a hugely flawed model for series TV. There is a natural audience attrition rate. People have lives and jobs and kids. You pin your entire series on requiring people to have seen the episode just before the one that's airing, but many people don't want to do that. You can get saddled by convoluted storytelling, wrapped so tightly that somebody on the outside can't get in.

LARRY: Does having DVR and DVD help mitigate that attrition?

TIM: Okay, I've gotten in trouble talking about this before, so let me articulate it properly. In regards to new technologies—they are great for fandom. They allow fans to watch what they want, when they want. However, for series television, these technologies are not good.

LARRY: Because they allow people to skip through, or avoid, the ads—and those ads fund the show. If people don't watch them, the advertisers don't want to pay so much.

TIM: Plus, you have the attrition rate with a serialized drama, and they don't rerun well.

LARRY: So here you are, working on a serialized drama, with high-level writers who had to suppress their egos, on an expensive show. What other challenges cropped up?

TIM: The truth is that it takes the unique writer's voice and limits it. There isn't a chance for that one offbeat writer to do an episode that is truly different. The highs and lows are clipped, simply by virtue of using a committee.

LARRY: Although as long as everyone is committed to the same vision of the show, then it'll smooth it out.

TIM: But even then, the vision was truly created by twelve people instead of one. Normally, the guy who creates the show has the vision. I've never been like that. I had an idea, and a feeling, and a sense of big ideas—but I did not have one hundred episodes of story. So finding that vision became tricky, and when you create something that you hand over to twelve people in a Room, you have to be prepared for it to become something different.

LARRY: Which goes back to ego. You have to let it go.

TIM: And it can be incredibly beautiful and exhilarating to watch something change into something better from all these voices. The drawback is you don't necessarily recognize the voice you had originally. The other issue is that things move so fast that if you aren't completely on board, it can quickly move further away from something you recognize.

LARRY: Which will happen because a showrunner is pulled in so many directions.

TIM: If I go into the editing room for thirty hours, then come back to the Writers' Room and hear all these pitches, and I don't like them, then I've detonated a week's worth of work. We cannot afford that loss of time. So I have to say, "Okay, we have to go in that direction" and go with it. I must wrap my brain around something that isn't mine. Be constructive, not destructive.

LARRY: You really have to be secure with your own talent, success, and ego to do that.

TIM: Yes, because it's like having a child, giving it up to a Chinese family for adoption, and seeing the child a year later—and the child speaks Chinese. It's my child, but I can't understand everything it's saying! But I still have this connection to it.

LARRY: This even extends to your crew.

TIM: We have four hundred people! And I have to allow them to put their fingers on it, or they won't show up at 5:00 a.m. and work eighteen hours. And so I give up ownership of it. I have to.

LARRY: It runs so contrary to the auteur theory of television.

TIM: I'm a racehorse and not a workhorse. I work by inspiration. I wait, sometimes very impatiently, for inspiration to strike. I can't churn stuff out like David Milch or David E. Kelley. I must enlist other people.

LARRY: Is this related to all the years you spent freelancing?

TIM: Definitely. I worked four or five different shows a year in wildly different genres, and it gave me a short attention span. I birth something, fall in love with it, and then walk away from it. I still have that tendency. I love these characters and live with them and give birth to them, and then they sort of die for me.

LARRY: It's hard to walk away.

TIM: I beat myself up over that sometimes: "Why are they dead for me?" But that's who I am. So *Heroes,* in its schizophrenic nature, is a reflection of my short attention span. That we can have wildly over-the-top melodrama and slapstick humor in one episode reflects this.

LARRY: The benefit of this, as a staff writer, is that I feel empowered. I feel my contribution matters, and that I'm helping you.

TIM: I wish I could say it was by design. But my dependence on other people, in a very open and revealing and vulnerable way, becomes a tool. People understand this about me—that I can go into their room and close the door and tell them, "I need five talking points for this network meeting, and I have no idea what to say." It makes them feel like, "Wow, Tim really needs me. He'd fall apart without me!" So, yeah, it's nice to know that you're needed.

LARRY: My own experience has not always reflected that state of mind, alas.

TIM: There are certain places where you work in fear, or try to be constructive, and get shot down. That doesn't happen here. But my approach has upsides and downsides. I create a scrum beneath me because I don't lay out a hierarchy. There's just so much work that people must jump in. It's "all hands on deck" from day one, like being in a foxhole.

LARRY: And yet do some people seek out a hierarchy? It's human nature.

TIM: I've been surprised that people like to be told what to do and know where they are in the hierarchy. They'd rather be lower down and know where they are than vie for the top spot.

LARRY: I wonder if that comes from the culture of fear that can pervade a staff? I want to know what's expected of me, and how not to piss you off. And if I'm told what's expected, then I can't get into trouble, whereas if it's a loose structure, I'm less secure.

TIM: When you are indoctrinated in the system and learn the transitory nature of your job, it's no wonder you end up that way. Because I wrote every freelance assignment as if I would win the Oscar, I never thought of a job as how it would advance me to the next rung within the staff hierarchy. I did not internalize those levels as being important.

LARRY: Let's talk about the audience impact on the show. When it became apparent that the show was a global hit, did you become concerned about how fans would react to things?

TIM: Yes and no. Because we are developing stories five episodes ahead of what the audience is watching, it's hard to react to them.

LARRY: Did it affect the creative process within the production?

TIM: Once you're a hit, there's a natural tendency to get cautious—a fear of screwing up what's working. But the bigger problem is that, like spoiled kids, you don't know where your limits are. So we had a Creeping Gigantus problem—things got bigger and louder, and more meant better. Bigger storylines, larger number of sets, more effects, and the show got too big and too crazy.

LARRY: Can you pinpoint when that started to happen?

TIM: The second season.

LARRY: A direct result of success?

TIM: Yes, the truth is we should never have done as many episodes as we did. That's the biggest problem with a show like this in the world of network TV. The storytelling is more precious. You have to protect and hone it. We have a tenuous relationship with viewers. So instead of giving the audience small bites and leaving them wanting more, we did twenty-five episodes in the third season. It felt more like an all-you-can-eat buffet rather than the tapas bar. Things are only rare and special if they're not around all the time. You can't create an event or a rareness if it's ubiquitous. And because of new technologies, the shelf life of a zeitgeist idea like *Heroes* is shorter and shorter. It's harder to sustain a phenom. And one thing that limits the shelf life is how much we're giving to people. I think we gave them too much.

LARRY: Did you have a sense of this Creeping Gigantus?

TIM: Yes, but we could not do much about it. It has a self-perpetuating inertia. So we really pulled things back in the second half of the third season. We went back to more character-based storytelling and relied less on pyrotechnics.

LARRY: When we first talked, you said that you hoped you'd be able to have characters come and go: some would die; others would take their place. That's not how things turned out. Was that an unexpected pitfall of the show's success?

TIM: Yes. It was a huge surprise. I was convinced the way to keep the show fresh was to keep doing origin stories. The problem is that the system isn't designed for that. It's designed for six-year actor contracts, and for actors who become the face of the show, and for the audience who fall in love with those characters, and so you must service those characters. When you bring in a new character, they are judged against the regulars. And some don't want to watch those new characters because they compete for screen time with the regulars they love. So it handcuffs you to telling stories over and over again with the same characters.

LARRY: And you start to stray from your original inspiration.

TIM: Exactly, and that can be creatively frustrating. Because once those characters are in full command of what was happening to them, all the existential questions that I found infinitely fascinating—"What's happening to me? How am I connected to these other people?"—these get replaced by plot questions. And because questions are what drives the show, that's when the show got less interesting. So we've tried to go back to these questions. It's why characters lost their powers, go back to their lives, and so on, so they can continue to have those questions.

LARRY: So you must be infinitely creative—to find ways of telling quasi-origin stories by having things occur like the eclipse. Suddenly everyone loses their powers.

TIM: You've identified the issues we really struggle with. It's a very complicated storytelling model. The serialized nature demands these inevitabilities. Characters have to change in serialized storytelling. If they don't, people think they're the same. But once they change, then they may not serve the same purpose anymore! And if you must still service them because they're under contract, then you're constantly changing what their purpose is, until they don't resemble what you initially wanted to say with them!

LARRY: Whereas on a procedural drama that's closed-ended each week, the characters don't have to change that much. Those shows instead rely on more intellectual questions or are driven more by an exploration of theme rather than character.

TIM: But the characters don't have to change as people.

LARRY: So with Sylar "becoming" Nathan at the end of Season 3—

TIM: Perfect example of the kind of contortionism we must do.

LARRY: But necessity is the mother of invention. Your restriction has generated a scenario with all kinds of possibilities.

TIM: Yes, that was an idea that has paid tremendous dividends.

LARRY: Are you still writing by character storyline, as you did in the first year?

TIM: Yes, we're going back to that. We had crept too much into each episode being written by one or two people.

LARRY: Seems to me that with this approach, the other pitfall is leaning too much on craft.

TIM: Writingwise, the show lends itself to multiple voices. I don't want this to sound negative, but *Heroes* is not a very "writerly" show. There's not much subtext. Very efficient storytelling. Very little banter. There's no need for it. It's not a show that has much downtime for the characters. Most characters say what's on their mind to move the story forward. So it doesn't really call for a unique voice. The upside is that most writers can write these characters, and as an audience member, you can't tell the difference.

LARRY: Once again, the writer must let go of their ego.

TIM: It's the sheer volume of work. It's so daunting. Someone says, "It's so much easier if you help me out with this! God, I need the help!"

LARRY: You mentioned that you write more as an ER doctor, fixing things, on this show.

TIM: I did write five full shows this past season. I do write on my own for those episodes. There are certain tonal things to address, and it's better for me to set that tone. But I don't do much rewriting. Tabling the script and everyone providing their input mitigate that process. I'll do a pass, but it's usually just trims and tweaks. It's about cutting page count down. It's surgical.

LARRY: Let's talk transmedia, which you really advanced in terms of integrating it into a network show. Is that content separate from the show, or integrated?

TIM: Very integrated. The transmedia angle is a separate but equal part of the show. Many stories have natural extensions to the Web. Things that maybe don't work for the network side might work great as an online comic. Or if we create someone online and bring him on the show, or vice versa, like the Web series we just did with the character of Doyle. It was hugely successful. Everything is vetted through the Writers' Room. When the writers went on strike, much of the online content continued without anyone from the show being involved, so we had to disavow it and say it was not part of the canon of the show.

LARRY: So again, another potential pitfall. Another thing a showrunner must keep his eye on.

TIM: You can get into some really dangerous territory. There's a thin line that connects the show with its fans—the thread of authenticity. That thread can be severed by any number of things, boneheaded or arrogant moves, or moves that are made by people who are not connected to the creative engine of the show. If some marketing intern gets some transmedia angle jammed into the mythology of the show without our approval, that can really screw things up.

Further Reading

Aristotle. Poetics. Edited by Malcolm Heath. London and New York: Penguin, 1996.

The Participants

Bibliography

Index

The Participants

Neal Baer

Dr. Neal Baer is executive producer of the NBC television series *Law & Order: Special Victims Unit*. During his tenure, the series has won the Shine Award, the Prism Award, and the Media Access Award, and has grown in both critical and popular stature. The series regularly appears among the top-ten television dramas in national ratings. Before his work on *SVU,* Dr. Baer was executive producer of the NBC series *ER.* A member of the show's original staff and a writer and producer on the series for seven seasons, he was nominated for five Emmys as a producer.

He also received Emmy nominations for Outstanding Writing in a Drama Series for the episodes "Hell and High Water" and "Whose Appy Now?" For the latter, he also received a Writers Guild of America nomination.

Dr. Baer's other work includes "Warriors," an episode of *China Beach,* nominated for a Writers Guild Award for Best Episodic Drama, and the *ABC Afterschool Special* "Private Affairs," which he directed and wrote. The Association of Women in Film and Television selected the program, dealing with sexually transmitted diseases, as the Best Children's Drama of the Year. He also recently wrote *The Doctor Corps,* a feature film for 20th Century Fox.

Dr. Baer graduated from Harvard Medical School and completed his internship in pediatrics at Children's Hospital, Los Angeles. He received the Jerry L. Pettis Memorial Scholarship from the American Medical Association as the most outstanding medical student who has contributed to promoting a better understanding of medicine in the media. The American Association for the Advancement of Science selected him as a Mass Media Fellow. In 2003 he was honored by Physicians for Social Responsibility, Lupus L.A., and the Media Project.

Dr. Baer's primary medical interests are in adolescent health. He has written extensively for teens on health issues for *Scholastic Magazine,* covering such topics as teen pregnancy, AIDS, drug and alcohol abuse, and nutrition. Dr. Baer taught elementary school in Colorado and also worked as a research associate at the University of Southern California Medical School, where he focused on drug- and alcohol-abuse prevention.

Dr. Baer graduated magna cum laude with a BA in political science from Colorado College. He holds master's degrees from Harvard Graduate School of Education and from Harvard Graduate School of Arts and Sciences in sociology. Before working in television, he spent a year at the American Film Institute as a directing fellow. In 2000 he received an honorary doctor of laws from Colorado College.

Dr. Baer serves on the boards of many organizations related to health care, including the Venice Family Clinic, RAND Health, Advocates for Youth, Children Now, the Huckleberry Fund of Children's Hospital–Los Angeles, and the National Organization on Fetal Alcohol Syndrome (NOFAS). He is a trustee of the Writers Guild of America Health and Pension Fund and a member of the Board of Associates at the Whitehead Institute for Biomedical Research.

Dr. Baer received the Valentine Davies Award for 2004 from the Writers Guild of America, West, for "public service efforts in both the entertainment industry and the community at large, bringing dignity to and raising the standard for writers everywhere." In 2003 he received the Special Individual Achievement Award from the Media Project, the Leadership Award from NOFAS, the Loop Award from Lupus L.A. for educating the public about lupus and autoimmune diseases, and the Socially Responsible Medicine Award from Physicians for Social Responsibility for "accomplishment in crafting compelling health messages." Dr. Baer lives in Los Angeles with his wife, Gerrie Smith, who is on the board of the service organization City Hearts, and his son Caleb, fourteen.

Carol Barbee

Three Rivers: Executive producer
Swingtown: Executive producer
Jericho: Executive producer
Judging Amy: Executive producer
Providence: Supervising producer

Chris Brancato

Chris Brancato is a Hollywood writer and producer of several films and television programs. Brancato grew up in Teaneck, New Jersey, and graduated from

Teaneck High School. He now lives in Los Angeles. He is the son of novelist Robin Brancato and teacher John Brancato.

Brancato wrote or was story editor for several episodes of the 1992 season of *Beverly Hills, 90210*. He wrote the *X-Files* episode "Eve," which first aired on December 10, 1993. Brancato created and wrote the Sci Fi Channel's *First Wave*, which aired from 1998 to 2001. He was co–executive producer of *Boomtown*, consulting producer on *Tru Calling*, and a frequent writer and executive producer of drama pilots.

Brancato also cowrote the 1998 film *Species II* and was executive producer of the 2002 film *Stealing Harvard*.

Dan Bucatinsky

> *Lipstick Jungle:* Consulting producer
> *The Comeback:* Executive producer
> *The Commuters:* Executive producer
> *Beck and Call:* Executive producer

Michael S. Chernuchin

Michael Chernuchin was the executive producer and head writer of NBC's long-running *Law & Order* as well as CBS's *Michael Hayes* (starring David Caruso) and *Brooklyn South*. He also created and executive produced the CBS drama *Feds* as well as TNT's first prime-time drama, *Bull*. For his work he has been distinguished with numerous awards, including the Peabody Award, the Edgar Allan Poe Award given by the Mystery Writers of America, the People's Choice Award, four Emmy nominations, three Writers Guild nominations for Best Dramatic Episode, a nomination for the Humanitas Prize for Best Dramatic Episode, the Angel Award for Best Dramatic Episode, the Jewish Televimage Award, the American Psychological Association Award, the American Cancer Society Award, and the George S. Felton Producer of the Year.

Chernuchin served as consulting producer on the first year of FOX's *24* and FOX's drama *Canterbury's Law* starring Julianna Margulies, and he returned to the *Law & Order* arena as co–executive producer of *Law & Order: Criminal Intent*.

In addition to his television work, he cowrote the feature film *Eraser* starring Arnold Schwarzenegger and has also completed a feature film for Kevin Costner's TIG Productions.

Before becoming a writer, Chernuchin was an attorney practicing in New York City. He received his JD from Cornell Law School where he served as an editor of the *Law Review,* his MA in English literature from the University of Michigan, and his AB from Dartmouth College.

Jane Espenson

Jane Espenson grew up in Ames, Iowa, where she watched too much television. At age thirteen she attempted to write an episode of *M*A*S*H.* It did not work out. She attended college at the University of California–Berkeley, studying linguistics as an undergraduate and graduate student. While in grad school she submitted spec episodes of *Star Trek: The Next Generation,* and got her tiny foot wedged in the last open door of show business. After winning a spot in the Walt Disney Writers' Fellowship, she worked in sitcoms for a number of years. Her first staff job at a drama was at *Buffy the Vampire Slayer,* followed by a year as co–executive producer at *Gilmore Girls* and brief stints as co–executive producer of the canceled FOX dramas *Tru Calling* and *The Inside.* She became co–executive producer for *Jake in Progress* and began a long stint with various forms of SciFi's *Battlestar Galactica.* Her work for that series included twenty episodes as co–executive producer, as well as being co–executive producer for the MOW *Battlestar Galactica: Razor* and its Internet incarnation, *Razor Flashbacks.* She also wrote and executive produced the Internet series *Battlestar Galactica: Face of the Enemy,* executive produced *Caprica,* and most recently served as consulting producer on Joss Whedon's *Dollhouse* for FOX.

Bryan Fuller

Bryan is a self-professed *Star Trek* geek who watched and loved the *Trek* series *Deep Space Nine* and set out to write for them. At the time *Star Trek* had an open script-submission policy, and Fuller contributed a spec, leading to a pitching opportunity. When he had sold a couple of stories to *Deep Space Nine,* Fuller was hired to be a full staff writer for sister *Trek* series *Voyager* in its fourth season. He worked on *Voyager* for the remainder of its seven-year run, working his way up to coproducer of the series. During the last year of *Voyager,* Fuller delivered the pilot spec for *Dead Like Me* to his agent, who immediately sold it. *Dead Like Me* was canceled after two seasons, but Fuller was a trusted commodity at this point and moved on to create the short-lived but critically acclaimed *Wonderfalls.*

Fuller has had a meteoric career in television and has worked nonstop since first pitching to *Deep Space Nine* in 1993. He wrote and produced an animated movie with Mike Mignola called *The Amazing Screw-On Head*. He then moved on to co–executive produce and write for *Heroes,* which became a smash hit. Even though the show was picked up for a second season, Fuller left to create his critically acclaimed new show, *Pushing Daisies,* returning to *Heroes* after ABC declined to renew *Daisies*.

Javier Grillo-Marxuach

Javier "Javi" Grillo-Marxuach writes and produces television shows, films, and comic books. Though best known for his work as writer and producer on the first two seasons of the Emmy- and Golden Globe–winning American Film Institute honoree *Lost,* he has also written for the Peabody Award–winning *Boomtown,* as well as *Medium, Charmed, The Pretender, The Chronicle, Jake 2.0, SeaQuest, Dark Skies,* and *Law and Order: Special Victims Unit*. He received a BA in 1991 from Carnegie Mellon and has an MFA from the University of Southern California.

In 2005 he entered the world of comics with his own Viper Comics title, *The Middleman*. He also created the Marvel Comics cosmic character *Wraith* and wrote the *Super-Skrull* limited series of the company's Annihilation event, as well as Dynamite Entertainment's four-issue limited-series classic *Battlestar Galactica: Cylon Apocalypse*.

In 2008 ABC Family picked up his television series based on his comic book series *The Middleman,* for which he was the executive producer and showrunner. He is currently rewriting a feature film in the horror genre and working on a pilot.

Hart Hanson

Bones: Executive producer
Joan of Arcadia: Consulting producer
Expert Witness: Executive producer
Judging Amy: Executive producer
Snoops: Co–executive producer
Cupid: Supervising producer
Traders: Supervising producer
Trust in Me: Associate producer

Aaron Harberts and Gretchen Berg

Mercy: Executive producer
Pushing Daisies: Co–executive producers
Women's Murder Club: Co–executive producers
Pepper Dennis: Executive producer
North Shore: Co–executive producers
Wonderfalls: Supervising producer
The Deerings: Executive producer
John Doe: Supervising producer
Roswell: Coproducers

Jason Katims

A writer with a background in New York theater, responsible for the plays *The Man Who Couldn't Dance, Driving Lessons,* and *Catch!* and the frequently produced one-act *Who Made Robert De Niro King of America?* Jason Katims brought his talents to television in the mid-1990s after being discovered by producer Edward Zwick.

He debuted with a writing credit in an episode of the short-lived 1994 CBS drama *The Road Home* before teaming up with Zwick and Marshall Herskovitz, the pair behind ABC's *thirtysomething,* to work on the teen drama *My So-Called Life* (ABC, 1994–95), an uncommonly realistic and finely scripted portrait of a teenage girl's navigation of everyday high school existence. A story editor on *My So-Called Life,* Katims penned three episodes of the series, the remarkable entries "The Substitute" and "Life of Brian" as well as the holiday-themed "So-Called Angels," featuring his father, actor Robert Katims, in a guest role. Although it received rave reviews and captured a fiercely loyal following, *My So-Called Life* (aired on Thursdays, up against NBC's unbeatable lineup) lasted only a half season on the network before retiring to cult status and extensive repeats on MTV.

In 1997, a year after he made his feature-writing and coproducing debut with the comparably unimpressive *The Pallbearer,* Katims returned to series television alongside Zwick and Herskovitz as creator of *Relativity.* A look at the advent of a romance between two twentysomethings from divergent backgrounds (she from upper-middle-class WASP stock, he the son of a blue-collar Jewish family), *Relativity* had all the emotional honesty and intensity of *My So-Called Life,* with a gen-erational-appropriate focus on interpersonal relationships with family, friends, and lovers. Although *Relativity* bore the marks of the awkward introspection and self-consciousness that *thirtysomething* was famous for, Katims's characters were decidedly more likable than the often irritating *thirtysomething* ensemble.

Following the imminent cancellation of *Relativity* after a brief but acclaimed run, Katims went in a different direction with the sci-fi teen drama *Roswell*. Well written and acted, *Roswell* earnestly followed the budding romance between Max (Jason Behr), an otherworldly being in human teenage form, and Liz (Shiri Appleby), his earthling classmate. This tried-and-true plot of opposites attracting injected some suspense into the proceedings, with Max and his two fellow aliens (Brendan Fehr and Katherine Heigl) struggling to keep the truth of their origins secret after Max jeopardizes their safety by using his powers to save Liz's life. The compelling series, yet another entry in the writer's impressive body of work, added a dimension of emotional and romantic realism to the science fiction genre. The alien theme separated it from the influx of teen-aimed series, showed Katims's versatility, and also ensured *Roswell* a larger audience, bringing in sci-fi enthusiasts who were not drawn to the writer's previous efforts.

Following *Roswell*, Jason went on to become the executive producer of *Boston Public* for four years and the executive producer of *Pepper Dennis* and *The Wedding Bells*. He is currently the executive producer of *Friday Night Lights,* which is about to enter its fourth season.

Tim Kring

Series
Chicago Hope: Producer, then supervising producer
L.A. Doctors: Co–executive producer
Strange World: Creator and executive producer
Providence: Co–executive producer
Crossing Jordan: Executive producer, showrunner, and creator
Heroes: Executive producer, showrunner, and creator
Screenplays
Teen Wolf Too
Sublet (also known as *Codename: Jaguar*)
Television Movies
Bay Coven (also known as *Bay Cove, Eye of the Demon, Strangers in Town,* and *The Devils of Bay Cove*)
Without Consent (also known as *Tell Laura I Love Her* and *Trapped and Deceived*)
Falling for You (CBS)

Peter Lenkov

Peter Lenkov is a TV and film writer and producer as well as an occasional writer of comic books. He was born in Montreal. He spent the first twenty-one years of his life in Chomedey, Laval (a Montreal suburb). He attended both McGill University and Concordia University. He is married to former model and actress Audie England. He currently resides on a ranch outside Los Angeles with his wife, three children, and his collection of animals: dogs, pigs, rabbits, chickens, horses, and donkeys.

Notable work includes the TV series *24* and *CSI: NY* and films such as *Demolition Man*. In comics he wrote *Fort: Prophet of the Unexplained*, for which he was nominated for the Bram Stoker Award for Best Illustrated Narrative. In 2003 he was nominated for an Emmy Award for his work on the hit TV series *24*. Other awards include a Media Access Award for his work on *CSI: NY* and a Huntington Disease Honor for an episode of *The District*.

Laurie McCarthy

Ghost Whisperer: Co–executive producer
Windfall: Executive producer
The Handler: Co–executive producer
CSI: Miami: Co–executive producer
Cover Me: Co–executive producer
Beverly Hills, 90210: Co–executive producer

Frank Military

The Handler: Producer
NCIS: Producer
Windfall: Supervising producer
Jericho: Supervising producer
The Unit: Co–executive producer
Three Rivers: Co–executive producer

Kim Newton

Kim Newton most recently served as co–executive producer and writer for CBS's *Eleventh Hour*. Newton was raised in both Los Angeles and Houston. She attended Texas State University, receiving a bachelor's degree in journalism and advertising. She worked as a copywriter for J. Walter Thompson in Dallas for three years before moving to Los Angeles with hopes of becoming a comedy writer. As luck would have it, Kim quickly secured a coveted position as a writers' assistant on David Kelley's first hit show, *Picket Fences,* where she was mentored by Ann Donahue of *CSI* fame. Her focus quickly switched to the one-hour drama.

Kim began her career with a speculative script sold to *Chicago Hope,* then staffed on *The X-Files.* Her credits include *The Fugitive, Fastlane, Cold Case,* and *Las Vegas,* among others.

Kim resides in Los Angeles with her son, Oscar.

Shawn Ryan

Shawn Ryan is a writer, showrunner, and producer; the creator of the acclaimed television series *The Shield;* and the showrunner of *The Unit.* He is a graduate of Middlebury College and is married to actress Cathy Cahlin Ryan, who also stars on *The Shield.* They have two children.

Ryan got his start in television as a staff writer on the show *Nash Bridges* and served as producer on *Angel* before creating *The Shield* and *The Unit.* He has also written for each show he has worked on. In commentary tracks on *The Shield* DVD sets, Ryan frequently credits his experiences on the earlier shows with giving him valuable experience for his own creations.

He is currently under an overall development deal with 20th Century Fox, where he is pursuing projects with other writers, including James Ellroy.

Robert Singer

In his long career Robert Singer has produced three feature films, the most notable being the 1983 Warner Brothers hit Stephen King's *Cujo.*

He has also executive produced nearly four hundred hours of network television, including *Lois & Clark: The New Adventures of Superman* and the Mark Harmon–Marlee Matlin series *Reasonable Doubts,* which Singer created. He also created the William Devane series *Turks* for Universal and *Charlie Grace* for Warner Brothers.

Singer has written and directed extensively for his own executive produced series, including the acclaimed *Midnight Caller,* starring Gary Cole. His prolific directing credits include the NBC two-hour movie *War Stories,* starring Jeff

Goldblum, in addition to numerous other pilots and series, including *American Dreams, Monk,* and *The Fugitive,* to name but a few.

Singer is currently working on the CW series *Supernatural* as executive producer and one of its principal directors.

Gardner Stern

Two-time Emmy Award–winning writer-producer Gardner Stern lent his creative talents to NBC's sexy hit drama *Las Vegas,* serving as executive producer and writer. Born and raised in Chicago, Stern attended Yale University, receiving a bachelor's degree in history before earning his master's degree in business administration at the University of Chicago. After a seven-year stint in the world of advertising, he made the transition to television, moving to Los Angeles and eventually beginning his television career as a staff writer on the drama *Capitol News.*

Stern's other writing and producing credits include NBC's *Law & Order, NYPD Blue, Chicago Hope,* and *The Practice.* He also created the critically acclaimed cable series *Breaking News.*

The recipient of two Peabody Awards, Stern also garnered a Golden Globe Award and two Emmy Awards for his work on *NYPD Blue.* He also received a Producers Guild of America Golden Laurel Award for his work on *Law & Order* and the Humanitas Prize.

Stern resides in Los Angeles with his wife and three children.

Vanessa Taylor

Tell Me You Love Me: Consulting producer
Jack & Bobby: Co–executive producer
Everwood: Producer
Alias: Coproducer

Bibliography

Television Shows, Films, and Music

Alf. NBC, 1986–90.

Alien. Directed by Ridley Scott. 20th Century Fox, 1979.

All My Children. ABC, 1970–present.

Barney Miller. ABC, 1975–82.

The Beachcombers. CBC, 1972–90.

Beverly Hills, 90210. FOX, 1990–2000.

Boomtown. NBC, 2002.

Boston Public. FOX, 2000–4.

Bull. TNT, 2000.

CSI. CBS, 2000–present.

Chicago Hope. CBS, 1994–2000.

Cupid. ABC, 1998–99.

Dark Shadows. ABC, 1966–71.

Deadwood. HBO, 2004–6.

Desperate Housewives. ABC, 2004–present.

Dinosaurs. ABC, 1991–94.

The District. CBS, 2000–4.

ER. NBC, 1994–2009.

Eternal Sunshine of the Spotless Mind. Directed by Michel Gondry. Focus, 2004.

Friday Night Lights. NBC, 2006–present.

Genesis. "That's All." *Genesis.* Atlantic, 1983.

Get Smart. CBS, 1965–70.

Hack. CBS, 2002–4.

Happy Days. ABC, 1974–84.

Heroes. NBC, 2006–present.

Hill Street Blues. NBC, 1981–87.

Homicide: Life on the Street. NBC, 1993–99.

The Incredibles. Directed by Brad Bird. Pixar, 2004.

Jack and Bobby. WB, 2004–5.

Knight Rider. NBC, 1982–86.

L.A. Law. NBC, 1986–94.

Las Vegas. NBC, 2003–8.

Law & Order: Special Victims Unit. NBC, 1999–present.

Lois & Clark: The New Adventures of Superman. ABC, 1993–97.

Lost. ABC, 2004–present.

Love Affair. Directed by Glenn Gordon Caron. Warner Brothers, 1994.

Miami Vice. NBC, 1984–89.

My So-Called Life. ABC, 1994–95.

My Two Dads. NBC, 1987–90.

Nash Bridges. CBS, 1996–2001.

Nowhere Man. UPN, 1995–96.

One Day at a Time. CBS, 1975–84.

Operation Petticoat. ABC, 1977–79.

Phenom. ABC, 1993.

Picket Fences. CBS, 1992–96.

SeaQuest. NBC, 1993–96.

Star Trek: The Next Generation. UPN, 1987–94.

Star Trek: Voyager. UPN, 1997–2001.

Star Wars. Directed by George Lucas. 20th Century Fox, 1977.

thirtysomething. ABC, 1987–91.

24. FOX, 2002–present.

The Unit. CBS, 2005–present.

V. NBC, 1984–85.

Vertigo. Directed by Alfred Hitchcock. Paramount, 1958.

Other Sources

de Vany, Arthur. 2003. *Hollywood Economics.* New York: Routledge.

Faulkner, William. 1950. "Nobel Prize Banquet Speech." Nobel Foundation, Stockholm, Dec.

Hemingway, Ernest. 1929. *A Farewell to Arms.* New York: Scribner.

Kaplan, Abraham. 1966. "The Aesthetics of the Popular Arts." *Journal of Aesthetics and Art Criticism* 24, no. 3 (Spring): 351–64.

Kurosawa, Akira. 1990. "1990 Academy Awards." Academy of Motion Picture Arts and Sciences, Los Angeles, Mar.

Mamet, David. 1991. *On Directing Film.* New York: Penguin.

———. 2007. *Bambi Meets Godzilla: On the Nature, Purpose, and Practice of the Movie Business.* New York: Pantheon Books.

Milch, David. 2007. "The Idea of the Writer." Writers Guild of America, Los Angeles, Dec.

Mills, Michael. 1998. "A Look at the Stanislavsky Method." Actors Studio.

Stanislavsky, Constantin. 1989. *An Actor Prepares.* Translated by Elizabeth Reynolds Hapgood. New York: Taylor and Francis.

Tolkien, J. R. R. 1973. *The Return of the King.* New York: Ballantine.

Index